Forensic Investigations

Using Science to Solve Crimes

BY
SCHYRLET CAMERON

COPYRIGHT © 2008 Mark Twain Media, Inc.

ISBN 978-1-58037-473-6

Printing No. CD-404098

Mark Twain Media, Inc., Publishers
Distributed by Carson-Dellosa Publishing LLC

Visit us at www.carsondellosa.com

Table of Contents

Introduction

Forensic Investigations: Using Science to Solve Crimes engages students in authentic science learning. Students explore the world of forensic science as they discover "whodunit" in each of the crime cases presented in this book. Students become crime scene investigators, examining clues, analyzing evidence, and interpreting data to identify the prime suspect.

Each "made-up" case is representative of a real-life middle-school situation. Student detectives gain an understanding of the difference between evidence and inference as they solve each case. There isn't one "correct" answer. This allows students to work like real forensic scientists: observing, experimenting, and discussing theories. The cases are purposefully designed to allow students to formulate different plausible solutions based on their interpretation of the evidence.

Forensic Investigations can be used to supplement current science curriculum, provide ideas for science fair projects, or energize your summer school program. Cases involve concepts and processes from different branches of science: inquiry science, earth science, life science, and physical science. The investigations in the book challenge students to actively combine science knowledge with reasoning and thinking skills. The activities provide students with many opportunities to practice the skills associated with the scientific method: observing, classifying, comparing, measuring, predicting, interpreting data, and drawing conclusions.

Each case contains the following sections:
- **Teacher Information** pages contain useful crime scene information, activities, and directions for the investigation. Suggested resources have been provided for further research or reference.
- A **Skill-Building Activity** introduces students to a specific skill that they will use to investigate the crime in each case.
- **Student Investigation** pages introduce the crime and guide students through the investigation and identification of the prime suspect.
- An **Analysis Lab** for each case provides students with the opportunity to apply the skills they have learned to analyze the evidence and come to a conclusion about "whodunit."

Forensic Investigations supports the No Child Left Behind Act. The investigations in this book promote student knowledge and understanding of science concepts. The inquiry-based activities are designed to strengthen scientific literacy skills and are correlated to the National Science Education Standards (NSES).

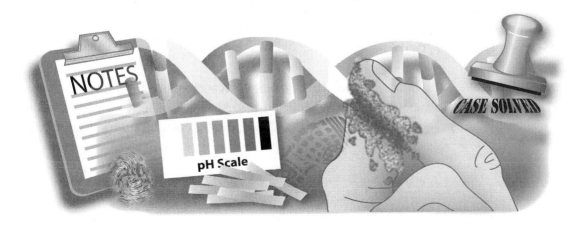

Using Science to Solve Crimes

Steps in Crime Investigation

A crime is like a giant jigsaw puzzle waiting to be solved. The police use science to put the pieces together to form a picture of what occurred at a crime scene. Many people are involved in gathering clues and searching for answers to solve the crime puzzle. One of the most important criminal investigative tools used by the police is the scientific method.

> **Scientific Method**
> Identify the Problem
> Collect Information
> Construct a Hypothesis
> Conduct Experiments
> Analyze Data
> Draw Conclusions

Step 1 Identify the Problem

Police officers are the first to arrive at the crime scene and identify the problem: a crime has been committed. They immediately secure the area by stretching yellow tape around the perimeter of the crime scene. The detectives and crime scene investigators arrive, put on plastic gloves, and walk through the crime scene together. They discuss various scenarios, identify items that might be evidence, and try to piece together what happened.

Step 2 Collect Information

Investigators look carefully at everything inside the perimeter of the crime scene. The smallest detail may help them piece together exactly what happened. Investigators carry crime scene kits containing everything they need to gather items from a crime scene: evidence bags to collect hairs and fibers; cotton swabs to save fluid samples; plastic tubes to store sand, dirt, or powder; and tweezers, pliers, scissors, and files to collect evidence when it cannot easily be picked up. Investigators record what the crime scene and evidence looks like by taking photographs and making sketches. The evidence is taken back to the forensic lab for closer examination and testing.

- **Physical evidence** is any items found at the crime scene or on victims such as DNA, fingerprints, footprints, or tire prints.
- **Trace evidence** is a very small amount of a material found at the crime scene or on victims such as hair, glass fragments, soil, or paint.

Step 3 Construct a Hypothesis

Detectives gather information about the crime by interviewing witnesses and victims. Using their research and the evidence found at the crime scene, detectives form a hypothesis: What crime took place? How was the crime committed? Who might be guilty of committing the crime?

Using Science to Solve Crimes (cont.)

Step 4 Conduct Experiments

Forensic scientists use various types of scientific equipment, including electronic microscopes, infrared photography, ultraviolet light, and X-ray machines, to examine physical and trace evidence found during a criminal investigation. Evidence is weighed, measured, and compared to reference files and computer databases.

Step 5 Analyze Data

Forensic scientists analyze data collected from the examination of the crime scene. They prepare reports that explain the results and describe the methods and techniques used to conduct the analysis.

The knowledge and experience of many different types of scientists may be needed to solve a crime.

- **Anthropologist:** examines and evaluates bones found at the crime scene to determine the identity of the victim and the way in which the person died
- **Biologist:** analyzes body fluids such as blood or saliva that have been left at the crime scene
- **Chemist:** analyzes substances found at the crime scene to determine if they contain chemicals (drugs or poisons)
- **Odontologist:** examines and evaluates dental evidence found at the crime scene to determine the identity of the victim or the offender
- **Entomologist:** examines insects at a crime scene to determine the time and location of the death of the victim
- **Geologist:** examines items such as soil, rock, sand, and minerals to determine where the crime was committed
- **Pathologist:** analyzes cells and tissues found at a crime scene and on a victim or suspect
- **Psychologist:** analyzes the behavior of people involved in the crime

Step 6 Draw Conclusions

Forensic science holds the key to solving the crime scene puzzle. Scientific principles and procedures are used to examine the evidence, obtain data, interpret results, and draw conclusions. The forensic scientist provides the detective with the information needed to determine the innocence or guilt of those accused and to solve the crime.

CSI Vocabulary

accomplice: a person connected with committing a crime

alibi: an account of where a suspect was or who they were with at the time of a crime

break-in: the illegal entrance into a premise with criminal intent

clue: a fact or an object that helps to solve a crime

crime: an act committed in violation of the law

criminal mischief: to damage, deface, or destroy someone's property

crime scene: the location where a crime has been committed

deduce: to infer by logical reasoning

detective: a person who investigates crimes and gathers information

evidence: an item used as proof in a crime

forensic science: the study of evidence in order to solve crimes and convict criminals

hunch: a feeling not based on known facts

investigation: the procedure of collecting evidence by law enforcement officers to solve a crime

investigator: a person who collects evidence to solve a crime

larceny: a minor theft

misdemeanor: a minor crime for which the punishment includes a fine and/or a maximum of one year of jail time

motive: the reason a person does something or acts in a certain way

offender: a person accused of a crime

perpetrator: a person who has allegedly committed a crime

petty larceny: to take something valued at less than $250.00

robbery: to take anything of value from a person by force, threat of force, or violence

suspect: a person thought to have committed a crime

trace evidence: anything found at a crime scene or on a victim in small but measurable amounts

victim: a person who is harmed or suffers some loss

witness: a person who saw or can give a firsthand account of a crime

Name: _____ Date: _____

CSI Crossword Puzzle

Use the clues below to complete the crossword puzzle.

ACROSS

2. the illegal entrance into a premises with criminal intent (hyphenated word)
6. an item used as proof in a crime
8. an account of where a suspect was or who they were with at the time of a crime
9. a person who has allegedly committed a crime
12. a feeling not based on known facts
13. a person connected with committing a crime
15. the reason a person does something or acts in a certain way
16. a fact or an object that helps to solve a crime
17. to take anything of value from a person by force, threat of force, or violence
18. a minor crime

DOWN

1. a person who collects evidence to solve a crime
3. a person accused of a crime
4. a person thought to have committed a crime
5. a person who is harmed or suffers some loss
7. a person who investigates crimes and gathers information
10. a minor theft
11. a person who saw or can give a firsthand account of a crime
14. an act committed in violation of the law

Science Vocabulary

classify: to use a system to group information into categories

conclusion: a summary of the results of the experimentation and a statement of how the results relate to the hypothesis

data: a group of measurements, facts, or statistics

data analysis: to organize and examine collected data using narratives, charts, graphs, or tables

experiment: the steps used to test a hypothesis

examine: to look closely at somebody or something

hypothesis: an idea about the solution to a problem that can be tested or investigated

identify: to name or recognize a person, place, or thing

laboratory: a place used for conducting scientific experiments

measure: a system of assigning numbers to an observation

observation: to use the senses to gather information about an object or event

predict: a forecast of future events based on previous observations and experiments

research: the method of collecting information and data about a topic being studied

science: the study of the natural world

scientific method: a series of steps scientists use to solve a problem

Name: _____ Date: _____

Science Word Search

Find and circle the words from the list below in the word search. Words may be printed horizontally, vertically, diagonally, forward, and backward.

```
A  N  A  L  Y  S  I  S  C  F  D  H  B  R  Y
H  C  R  A  E  S  E  R  O  Z  N  A  Z  E  R
S  W  R  J  U  F  B  X  N  J  G  D  T  E  O
I  F  M  B  V  B  B  T  C  H  P  T  X  A  T
S  S  C  I  E  N  C  E  L  L  E  P  D  Y  A
P  C  R  I  B  I  D  G  U  K  E  C  Q  M  R
Y  B  I  D  D  A  O  H  S  R  Q  U  A  Y  O
O  B  S  E  R  V  A  T  I  O  N  Q  F  E  B
T  I  R  N  N  Z  E  M  O  I  V  I  U  R  A
V  P  I  T  S  T  E  N  N  V  S  U  L  U  L
J  Y  I  I  J  N  I  K  I  S  P  E  N  S  D
G  D  I  F  T  S  Q  F  A  M  V  W  Q  A  R
S  L  J  Y  D  N  U  L  I  L  A  W  S  E  F
M  F  L  B  W  N  C  O  S  C  D  X  G  M  Y
S  I  S  E  H  T  O  P  Y  H  I  H  E  W  A
```

ANALYSIS	CLASSIFY	CONCLUSION
DATA	EXAMINE	EXPERIMENT
HYPOTHESIS	IDENTIFY	LABORATORY
MEASURE	OBSERVATION	PREDICT
RESEARCH	SCIENCE	SCIENTIFIC

Case #1
Forgery

Teacher Information

Crime Location: A middle-school science classroom is the crime scene.

Crime: Someone forged a field trip permission slip.

Investigation: Students compare the similarities and differences in handwriting samples.

Time Required: The student investigation takes approximately one 50-minute session to complete.

Materials Needed

* magnifying glasses
* a set of the Student Investigation pages for each team member

Teacher Notes

1. <u>Skill-Building Activity:</u> Instruct students to write the following sentence on unlined paper: "Every person has a unique style of handwriting." Students can use the information found on the Handwriting Characteristics page to analyze their own handwriting.

2. <u>Crime Scenario:</u> Students read and discuss the Crime Scene, Suspect Information, and Investigation Directions found on the Forgery page.

3. <u>Investigation:</u> Divide the class into teams. Instruct each team to complete the Handwriting Lab page using the permission note and the suspect's handwriting found on the Handwriting Samples page.

4. <u>Solve the Crime:</u> Students use the evidence to identify the prime suspect. Teams present their conclusions. There isn't one "correct" answer. The cases are purposely designed to allow students to formulate different plausible solutions based on their interpretation of the evidence.

NSES Science as Inquiry: Content Standard A:
As a result of activities in grades 5–8, all students should develop abilities necessary to do scientific inquiry.

Resources

<www.fbi.gov/fbikids.htm>
    ("Kids Page." <u>Federal Bureau of Investigation.</u> U.S. Department of Justice.)

Lowe, Shelia R. *The Complete Idiot's Guide to Handwriting.* Alpha Books, 1999.

Handwriting Characteristics

How each person learns to hold a pencil, form letters, and space words results in every person developing a unique style of handwriting. For this reason, handwriting analysis is a tool used by forensic scientists to detect forged documents.

The police often collect handwriting samples, or exemplars, when they believe forgery is involved in a case. A forensic document examiner is a handwriting expert. An examiner usually looks at the writing characteristics called traits. Traits include letter formation, size, and slant. The expert compares the key points of each trait found in the suspicious document to the exemplars.

Handwriting Traits

Forensic scientists analyze the key points of each handwriting trait when examining written documents. Some examples of handwriting traits and key points are illustrated in the table below.

TRAITS	KEY POINTS		
Baseline	Up *crime scene*	Down *crime scene*	Straight *crime scene*
Slant of Letters	Right *handwriting*	Left *handwriting*	Straight *handwriting*
Letter Size	Large *letters*	Medium *letters*	Small *letters*
Word Spacing	Close Together *keypoints*	Wide apart *key points*	Normal *key points*
Letter Formation "i"	Dots "i"	Does Not Dot "i"	Stylized "i"
Letter formation "t"	Cross "t"	Does Not Cross "t"	Stylized "t"
Letter Formation "r"	Angle "r" to Point	Flat-topped	Stylized "r"
Letter formation "e"	Looped "e"	Not Looped "e"	Stylized "e"

Name: _____ Date: _____

Handwriting Lab
Skill-Building Activity

Purpose: identify the handwriting traits found in the different writing samples

Materials Needed: an assortment of ink pens

Procedure:
Step 1: Each team member selects a different writing pen. Using cursive writing, each member copies the sample sentence in the correct space provided on the table.
Step 2: Examine the handwriting samples with a magnifying glass. Use the information found on the Handwriting Characteristics page to identify the traits found in the different writing samples.

Every person has a unique style of handwriting.
Team Member #1
Team Member #2
Team Member #3
Team Member #4
Team Member #5

Conclusion (Identify at least two traits of each handwriting sample.)

_____

_____

_____

Forgery
Student Investigation

Crime Scene

As the tardy bell rings, Kathy quickly hands her field trip permission note to her science teacher. Mrs. Brown glances at the note. She notices the handwriting looks more like a student's writing than an adult's writing. Mrs. Brown tucks the note in her pocket.

After class, Mrs. Brown walks to the office and presents the principal with the suspicious note. When Mr. Blackwell is unable to contact Kathy's parents, he calls Kathy into the office for a chat. After questioning, Kathy admits that one of her friends wrote the note. Kathy refuses to name the friend. Mr. Blackwell calls several of Kathy's friends to his office. He instructs Kathy as well as each of the other students to copy the permission note on an index card. The principal then compares the handwriting on the cards to the permission note. Who is guilty of forgery?

Suspect Information

1. Kathy is an honor roll student at Lincoln Middle School.
2. Jordan lives near Kathy. He looks forward to walking home with Kathy after school.
3. Amber is Kathy's best friend. She would do anything to help a friend.
4. Chelsea is new this year. She is shy and finds it hard to make friends. She is glad to be accepted by Kathy and her friends.
5. Reilly is Kathy's study buddy. Reilly is getting a low grade in science and needs Kathy's help studying for the next test.

Investigation Directions

Parents often communicate with the school through handwritten notes. Unfortunately, notes can be forged. You will use handwriting analysis to determine who wrote the permission note.

Step 1: Use a magnifying glass to examine the handwriting samples and permission note.
Step 2: Analyze each handwriting sample and the permission note using the Handwriting Characteristics page.
Step 3: Complete the Handwriting Lab page.
Step 4: Use the information from your investigation to identify the prime suspect.

Permission Note:

Kathy has my permission to go on the science field trip
                                          Mrs. Kilby

Handwriting Samples

Directions: When giving handwriting samples, criminals often try to disguise their writing. Even so, their handwriting will contain many similar features. Examine the handwriting samples with a magnifying glass. Note the key points of each trait, such as letter formation, spacing, slant, and baseline.

Permission Note:

Kathy has my permission to go on the science field trip
Mrs. Kilby

Suspect #1:   Kathy

Kathy has my permission to go on the science field trip.
Mrs. Kilby

Suspect #2:   Jordan

Kathy has my permission to go on the science field trip.
Mrs Kilby

Suspect #3:   Amber

Kathy has my permission to go on the science field trip.
Mrs. Kilby

Suspect #4:   Chelsea

Kathy has my permission to go on the science field trip.
Mrs. Kilby

Suspect #5:   Reilly

Kathy has my permission to go on the science field trip
Mrs Kilby

Name: _____ Date: _____

Handwriting Analysis Lab

Directions: Compare the permission note and each of the handwriting samples. Complete the table. Use the key point words located on the Handwriting Characteristics page to identify the traits found in the different writing samples.

Trait	Permission Note	Suspect #1: Kathy	Suspect #2: Jordan	Suspect #3: Amber	Suspect #4: Chelsea	Suspect #5: Reilly
Baseline						
Slant						
Size						
Spacing						
"i"						
"t"						
"r"						
"e"						

Whodunit?

Who is the prime suspect in the forgery case? Use evidence and details from the investigation to support your conclusion.

_____

_____

_____

_____

Case #2
Deception

Science Skills
classify
compare
predict
interpret data
draw inferences

Teacher Information
Crime Scene: A middle-school gymnasium is the scene of a crime.
Crime: Someone's behavior causes an accident.
Investigation: Students solve a crime by interpreting the body language displayed by suspects.
Time Required: The student investigation takes approximately two 50-minute sessions to complete.

Materials Needed
- a set of the six Truth or Deception cards
- a set of the Deception Student Investigation pages for each team

Teacher Notes
1. <u>Skill-Building Activity:</u> Guide students through the body language activity on the Truth or Deception page.
2. <u>Crime Scenario:</u> Students read and discuss the Crime Scene, Suspect Information, and Investigation Directions found on the Deception page.
3. <u>Investigation:</u> Divide the class into teams. Instruct each team to use the information found on the Investigation Report and Nonverbal Communications pages to analyze each suspect's body language.
4. <u>Solve the Crime:</u> Students use the evidence to identify the prime suspect. Teams present their conclusions. There isn't one "correct" answer. The cases are purposely designed to allow students to formulate different plausible solutions based on their interpretations of the evidence.

NSES Science as Inquiry: Content Standard A:
As a result of activities in grades 5–8, all students should develop abilities necessary to do scientific inquiry.

Resources
<http://members.aol.com/nonverbal2/diction1.htm#The%20NONVERBAL%20DICTIONARY>
("The Nonverbal Dictionary of Gestures, Signs, and Body Language Cues," Center for Nonverbal Studies.)

Harris, Elizabeth Snoke. *Crime Scene: Science Fair Project.* Lark Books, 2006.

Nonverbal Communication

A deceptive person is usually worried that they might be caught in a lie. They unknowingly send subconscious signals to the crime investigator. Subconscious signals refer to the nonverbal communication or body language that a suspect displays during questioning.

Signs of Deception

Body Part	Signs of Deception	Example
Eyes	• Avoids eye contact • Blinks often • Dilated pupils	
Mouth	• Twitching muscles • Licking lips • Chewing lips	
Hands	• Hiding hands • Fidgeting with hands or jewelry • Scratching nose or behind ear • Touching face	
Arms	• Crossing arms over chest	

Truth Or Deception
Skill-Building Activity

Students become "lie detectors" by observing how people move or use gestures when trying to deceive investigators.

Procedure:

Step 1: Duplicate and cut apart the six Truth and Deception cards.

Step 2: Select six student volunteers. Instruct the volunteers to stand in front of the class. They each select one of the cards from the Truth or Deception deck. Explain to the volunteers that they will be asked a question. If their card says "Truth," they should answer truthfully. If their card says "Deception," they should try to mislead the class by making up an answer to the question.

Question: Have you ever thrown a spit wad in class? If the answer is yes, describe the incident. If the answer is no, explain why you would not throw spit wads.

Step 3: Instruct the remaining students to observe and record the reactions of each student as they are being questioned: eye movement, hand motions, and posture.

Step 4: Students discuss their observations and identify the volunteers they believe to be telling the truth. The volunteers present their cards allowing students to check their conclusions.

Truth	Deception	Truth
Deception	Truth	Deception

Name: _____ Date: _____

Truth Or Deception Data Sheet
Skill-Building Activity

Directions: Observe each volunteer's reaction to the question: eye movement, hand motions, and posture. Analyze their behavior using the information found on the Nonverbal Communication page. Record your observation under the column labeled Signs of Deception. In the Truth or Deception column, write *truth* if you believe the volunteer was telling the truth. Write *deception* if you believe the volunteer was not being truthful.

Volunteer	Signs of Deception	Truth or Deception
Volunteer # 1		
Volunteer # 2		
Volunteer # 3		
Volunteer # 4		
Volunteer # 5		
Volunteer # 6		

How could body language be used by the police to solve a crime?

_____

_____

_____

_____

Deception
Student Investigation

Crime Scene

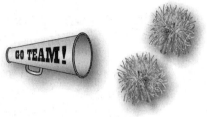

More than 400 boisterous spectators crammed into the Jefferson Middle School gym for the regional Cheerleader and Dance Association Championship. Twenty-five squads were waiting to tumble, cheer, and dance in one of the biggest cheerleading competitions in the area.

One by one, the crowd watched each squad perform carefully choreographed dance routines. Finally, the Jefferson Middle School squad took to the large red mat to perform in front of a cheering hometown crowd. The squad had invested hundreds of hours, tons of effort, and lots of hard-earned money in competing. They quickly launched into a flurry of cartwheels and jumps. It looked like they had the competition beat and would be heading for the National Championship. The crowd roared as fourteen-year-old Ashley Field was lifted and tossed into the air to perform a double flip. A gasp erupted from the spectators when a box of popcorn came flying out of the stands, hitting one of the cheerleaders who was supposed to catch Ashley. The crowd fell silent as Ashley tumbled out of control, falling through her teammate's arms and hitting the mat with a loud thud. Ashley was transported by ambulance to the local hospital. Who was responsible for the accident?

Suspect Information

1. Jessica is a student at Jefferson Middle School. She was seen running from the gym after the accident.
2. Tom is a student at Jefferson Middle School. He was sitting in front of Jessica during the competition, eating popcorn with his friends.
3. Kim is Ashley's best friend and teammate. They had worked for weeks perfecting the double flip. The girls had a heated argument about the routine before the competition.
4. Mrs. Evans is a mother of a cheerleader from one of the competing squads. She was sitting in the same bleacher section as Jessica and Tom.

Investigation Directions

The number one reason people lie is to avoid punishment. Nonverbal communication or body language can often tell police when a person is trying to deceive them.

Step 1: Read the Investigation Report and Nonverbal Communication pages.
Step 2: Record the signs of deception displayed by each suspect during the investigation on the Body Language Lab page.
Step 3: Use the evidence from your investigation to identify the prime suspect.

Investigation Report

Suspect Statements

People suspected of a crime are asked to give a statement. The statement often reveals the suspect's connections with the crime, where they were at the time of the crime, and a possible motive for committing the crime.

Jessica: "I sat on the second row of the bleachers directly in front of the performing cheerleaders. I admit that I despise cheerleaders. They are fake "rah-rah" girls who have nothing better to do than wear short skirts to show off their legs. But I didn't throw the popcorn."

Tom: "I sat in front of Jessica during the competition. The girls on the team are mean and snobby. I asked Ashley to the middle-school dance. She just laughed at me. I didn't see who threw the popcorn."

Kim: "Ashley is my best friend. I would never do anything to hurt her. My job was to catch Ashley when she did the double flip. When the popcorn hit me, it distracted me. That's why I didn't catch her."

Mrs. Evans: "My family wanted a good seat for the competition. We sat on the front row directly behind the judging table. The competition is very important to my daughter's future. Winning the regional Cheerleader and Dance Association Championship could help her get a college scholarship. I didn't see who threw the popcorn, but it wasn't me."

Investigator Notes

Good investigators lead the suspect to reveal if they committed a crime without directly asking the suspect if they are guilty. Investigators look for nonverbal clues, such as body language, to figure out if a suspect is being truthful.

Suspect #1: Jessica quickly entered the interrogation room and sat down. She kept her hands out of view under the table. She often licked her lips and avoided looking directly at anyone in the room when questioned.

Suspect #2: Tom slowly walked into the interrogation room. He looked around and then sat in the empty chair at the table. He placed his hands on top of the table. He looked directly at the investigators when questioned, but he often paused for several seconds before answering a question.

Suspect #3: Kim fidgeted with her bracelet as she entered the room. She walked to the table in the center of the room and sat down. She held both hands together in her lap during the questioning.

Suspect #4: Mrs. Evans confidently walked into the interrogation room. She paused for a few seconds, and then walked to the empty chair. She stood until the detective asked her to be seated. During the questioning, the detective noticed that Mrs. Evans tucked several stray strands of hair behind her ear and nervously touched a mole on her cheek.

Name: _____ Date: _____

Body Language Anaylsis Lab

Directions: Analyze the suspect's body language using the information found on the Investigation Report and Nonverbal Communication pages. Complete the table. Record the signs of deception displayed by each suspect.

Signs of Deception	Suspect #1: Jessica	Suspect #2: Tom	Suspect #3: Kim	Suspect #4: Mrs. Evans
Eyes				
Mouth				
Hands				
Arms				
Other Clues				

Whodunit?

Who is the prime suspect in the deception case? Use evidence and details from the investigation to support your conclusion.

_____

_____

_____

_____

Case #3
Theft

Teacher Information

Science Skills
classify
compare
predict
interpret data
draw inferences

Crime Location: The middle-school locker room is the crime scene.

Crime: Someone stole money and personal items from the boys' locker room.

Investigation: Students compare the similarities and differences in fingerprints.

Time Required: The student investigation takes approximately two 50-minute sessions to complete.

Materials Needed
- magnifying glasses, clear tape, and hand wipes
- Skill-Building Activity pages and Student Investigation pages for each student

Teacher Notes
1. Skill-Building Activity: Guide students through the Fingerprint Forensics and Analyzing Your Fingerprints Lab activity.
2. Crime Scene Scenario: Students read and discuss the Crime Scene, Suspect Information, and Investigation Directions found on the Theft: Student Investigation page.
3. Investigation: Divide the class into teams. Instruct each team to read and discuss the information found on the Investigation Report page. Next, they use the information found on the Fingerprint Forensics page to analyze the crime scene and suspects' fingerprints. Students record their findings on the Fingerprint Analysis Lab page.
4. Solve the Crime: Students use the evidence to identify the prime suspect. Teams present their conclusions. There isn't one "correct" answer. The cases are purposely designed to allow students to formulate different plausible solutions based on their interpretations of the evidence.

NSES Science as Inquiry: Content Standard A:
As a result of activities in grades 5–8, all students should develop abilities necessary to do scientific inquiry.

NSES Life Science: Content Standard C:
As a result of activities in grades 5–8, all students should develop an understanding of reproduction and heredity.

Resources
<http://www.fbi.gov/hq/cjisd/takingfps.html>
("Taking Legible Fingerprints," U.S. Department of Justice.)

Rollins, Barbara B. and Michael Dah. *Forensics Crime Solvers: Fingerprinting Evidence.* Coughlan Publishing, 2004

Fingerprint Forensics
Skill-Building Activity

Look closely at your fingertips with a magnifying glass. Each finger is covered with tiny ridges that form a unique pattern. You inherited this pattern from your parents. This pattern is your fingerprint. No two people have the same fingerprint pattern. This is why fingerprinting is an important tool used in crime scene investigations.

Three Types of Fingerprints

Plain Arch   Loop   Plain Whorl

Possible Variations of the Three Types of Fingerprints

Double Loop Whorl   Tented Arch   Accidental Whorl

Fingerprint comparisons can help investigators solve crimes. The police collect fingerprint evidence from suspects, victims, and the crime scene. Fingerprint examiners compare the prints to those saved on file or computer databases.

Types of Fingerprints:
- *Patent prints* are fingerprints that can be seen with the naked eye. Fingers that have dirt, blood, ink, or paint on them leave patent prints.
- *Latent prints* are fingerprints that are invisible. Investigators use several methods, such as dusting with powder, lasers or a strong light source, and heated super glue to make the prints visible.
- *Plastic prints* are fingerprints that leave an impression in soft objects: soap, wet cement, clay, or wax.

Collecting Fingerprints
- Investigators collect prints from crime scenes by dusting surfaces for latent prints, taking photographs of patent prints, and collecting soft objects with visible plastic prints.
- Police officers often take fingerprints from suspects and victims by rolling each finger over an ink pad. Then each finger is pressed onto a paper fingerprint card.
- Some police stations are equipped to take electronic pictures of fingerprints.

Name: _____ Date: _____

Analyzing Your Fingerprints Lab
Skill-Building Activity

Directions:

Step 1: Using a pencil, shade in the Fingerprint Pad box at right with even, dark strokes.

Step 2: Beginning with your right thumb, gently rub the surface of each fingertip over the shaded Fingerprint Pad (Prints may smudge if you rub too hard).

Step 3: Press a piece of clear tape on your fingertip. Gently lift the tape off your finger and tape it to the right thumb box of the Fingerprint Chart. Repeat for each finger.

Step 4: Examine each fingerprint with a magnifying glass. Use the Fingerprint Forensics page to determine which type of prints you have: loop, whorl, or arch. Record the information on the Fingerprint Chart. Look for any identifiable features, such as the directions of loops (right or left), double loops, or scars.

Fingerprint Chart

Right Hand

Thumb	Index Finger	Middle Finger	Ring Finger	Little Finger
Type:	Type:	Type:	Type:	Type:
Thumb	Index Finger	Middle Finger	Ring Finger	Little Finger
Type:	Type:	Type:	Type:	Type:

Left Hand

Theft
Student Investigation

Crime Scene

It's Homecoming! The steady beat of the Mountain Grove Middle School's victory song could be heard in the background. Parents, students, and community football fans exploded with jubilation. The Tiger's head coach, Kip Freeman, proudly signaled for his winning team to head to the locker room. The players rushed off the field, looking forward to the big celebration. Entering the locker room, they were shocked to find locker doors standing open, sports bags in disarray, and their personal items littering the floor. After a quick check, a number of players reported items missing.

Detectives investigating the break-in noticed that the stolen items would be difficult to trace: money, electronic devices, and clothing. Crime scene investigators took photographs and dusted for prints on lockers and the vinyl handles of the sports bags. The dusting revealed two prints. The investigators lifted the prints with tape and placed them on fingerprint cards. Later, at the forensic lab, a fingerprint examiner studied the prints and compared them to the fingerprints taken from the suspects identified by the detectives. Who is responsible for the locker room theft?

Suspect Information

1. Steve is an eighth-grade student at Mountain Grove Middle School who did not make the football team.
2. Mrs. Lee is the Mountain Grove Middle School night custodian and cleans up after every home game.
3. Mrs. Miller is president of the Mountain Grove Middle School Booster Club. Her son was replaced as quarterback after the last game because of his poor sportsmanship.
4. Kaylee is an eighth-grade student at Mountain Grove Middle School and a nominee for Homecoming Queen.

Investigation Directions

Each person has a unique set of fingerprints. When people touch objects with their fingers, a print is left behind. Fingerprints are one of the most important types of evidence collected by investigators from a crime scene. You will use fingerprint analysis to determine who is responsible for the locker room theft.

Step 1:   Read the Investigation Report page.
Step 2:   Complete the Fingerprint Analysis Lab page.
Step 3:   Use the information from your investigation to identify the prime suspect.

Investigation Report

Suspect statements

People suspected of a crime are asked to give a statement. The statement often reveals the suspect's connection with the crime, where they were at the time of the crime, and a possible motive for committing the crime.

Steve: "A bunch of skaters from the neighborhood meet after school to ride our skateboards in the faculty parking lot. It's not a big deal until there's a game. Every time there is a game, we get kicked off the school grounds."

Mrs. Lee: "Regardless of what some people may think, the school custodians do more than mop floors and take out garbage. I often work "security detail," providing assistance at after-school events and keeping an eye out for suspicious activity on the school grounds."

Mrs. Miller: "Our Booster Club members include players, parents, alumni, and friends; all of whom make up the Tiger Football Family. The primary purpose of our organization is to provide financial and emotional support for the players, even if we disagree with the coaching staff's decisions."

Kaylee: "The eighth-grade Homecoming Queen and King were going to be crowned tonight. Although I hadn't planned to attend the coronation or the dance, I think it is really sad the celebration had to be canceled."

Investigator's Notes

A detective locates and questions witnesses about persons seen or believed to have been in the area at the time of the crime. Observations, descriptions, and identifications made by witnesses can be useful in solving a crime. Investigators evaluate a witness's information and compare it with all the related data they have gathered.

Witness #1: "I saw Mrs. Miller standing in the school parking lot just before the game. She was waving her arms and yelling at several students holding skateboards."

Witness #2: "Fourth quarter, several students were horsing around and spilled a soda in front of the boy's locker room. Mrs. Lee cleaned up the mess."

Witness #3: "The names of the Homecoming Queen and King were announced today. I overheard Kaylee complaining, 'Looks count. If you're not model-thin, wear trendy clothes, and date a member of the football team, you don't have a chance at this school.'"

Name: _____ Date: _____

Fingerprint Analysis Lab

Directions: Examine the fingerprint evidence using the information found on the Fingerprint Forensics page. Identify each fingerprint type: loop, whorl, or arch. Record the information on the table. Look for any identifiable features, such as the direction of loops (right or left), double loops, or scars, and record the information. Analyze each of the prints to determine which samples taken from the suspects match the prints from the crime scene.

Fingerprint	Index Finger	Type of Print	Features
Crime Scene Print #1			
Crime Scene Print #2			
Suspect #1: Steve			

Name: _____ Date: _____

Fingerprint Analysis Lab (cont.)

Suspect #2: Mrs. Lee			
Suspect #3: Mrs. Miller			
Suspect #4: Kaylee			

Whodunit?

Who is the prime suspect in the theft case? Use evidence and details from the investigation to support your conclusion.

_____

_____

_____

_____

Case #4
Criminal Mischief

Teacher Information

Science Skills
classify
compare
predict
interpret data
draw inferences

Crime Location: The middle-school outdoor classroom is the crime scene.

Crime: Someone or something destroyed the outdoor classroom.

Investigation: Students compare the similarities and differences in animal prints.

Time Required: The student investigation takes approximately two 50-minute sessions to complete.

Materials Needed
- Skill-Building activity pages and Student Investigation pages for each student
- styrofoam blocks, art foam, ink pen, scissors, stamp pad, glue, and butcher paper

Teacher Notes
1. <u>Skill-Building Activity:</u> Guide students through the Mammal Track Characteristics, Animal Tracking Guide, and the Animal Stamps activity pages.
2. <u>Crime Scenario:</u> Students read and discuss the Crime Scene, Suspect Information, and Investigation Directions found on the Criminal Mischief Student Investigation page.
3. <u>Investigation:</u> Divide the class into teams. Instruct each team to read and discuss the information found on the Investigation Report page. Next, they use the information found on the Mammal Track Characteristics and Animal Tracking Guide pages to identify the crime scene prints. Students record their data on the Mammal Track Analysis Lab page.
4. <u>Solve the Crime:</u> Students use the evidence to identify the prime suspect. Teams present their conclusions. There isn't one "correct" answer. The cases are purposely designed to allow students to formulate different plausible solutions based on their interpretations of the evidence.

NSES Science as Inquiry: Content Standard A:
As a result of activities in grades 5–8, all students should develop abilities necessary to do scientific inquiry.

NSES Life Science: Content Standard C:
As a result of activities in grades 5–8, all students should develop an understanding of reproduction and heredity.

Resources
<http://www.biokids.umich.edu/guides/tracks_and_sign/tracks_key/tracks_mammal/>
    ("Mammal Tracks," University of Michigan)

Murie, Olaus and Roger Tory Peterson. *A Field Guide to Animal Tracks.* Houghton Mifflin, 1998.

Mammal Track Characteristics
Skill-Building Activity

Wherever mammals live, they produce evidence of their presence. This evidence is most commonly seen in the form of footprints or tracks found in soft, damp soil, mud, sand, or snow. Biologists look for three characteristics when identifying tracks: the shape of the print, the number of toes, and evidence of claws. Perfectly formed tracks are rarely found.

Characteristics	Examples
Two toes or hooves	• deer: prints measure 1–3 inches (2.54–7.62 cm) long • elk: prints measure 3–5 inches (7.62–12.7 cm) long
Four toes on front foot Four toes on hind foot	• the dog family (fox, wolf, coyote, neighborhood dog): prints show four toes on the front and rear feet • cat family (bobcat, lynx, neighborhood cat): retract their claws when they walk or run, so it is unusual to find claw marks with prints • rabbit family: most distinctive feature is the much longer rear feet
Four toes on front foot Five toes on hind foot	• rodent family (mice, chipmunks, squirrels, porcupine): hind tracks are usually placed side by side, hopping pattern, toes have bulbous tips, and the overall track is relatively round and symmetrical
Five toes on front foot Five toes on hind foot	• raccoon: elongated toes on all feet, front toes are open and hand-like • skunk: elongated toes on all feet • opossum: elongated front toes, rear hand-like track, there is often a tail mark running between the tracks
Prints with claw marks	• raccoons, skunks, coyotes, foxes, dogs: claw marks on front and back prints • rabbits: sometimes claws appear on rear toe prints

Animal Tracking Guide
Skill-Building Activity

  Wildlife can be found almost everywhere, even in densely populated urban areas. The most visible urban wildlife species include birds, squirrels, rats, mice, raccoons, rabbits, deer, bats, foxes, and opossums. Urban wildlife have adapted to the changes in their environment, and as a result, they sometimes become a nuisance to humans. They often snack on trees and shrubs, dig holes in lawns and flower beds, and leave droppings on playgrounds and ball fields.

  Wild animals can be difficult to detect in the urban setting because of their instinctive behavior to avoid humans. However, the presence of wild animals can be determined by the tracks they leave behind. The following illustrations are designed to help identify various species of animals by examining examples of their tracks. Special attention should be paid to characteristics such as shape of the track, number of toes, and presence or absence of claw marks.

fox	coyote	deer	raccoon
cat	pigeon	chipmunk	skunk
dog	rabbit	squirrel	opossum

Animal Stamps
Skill-Building Activity

Procedure:

Step 1: Choose an animal track from the Animal Tracking Guide page. Draw the outline of the animal track on paper. Cut out the pattern. Trace it onto art foam.

Step 2: Cut out the pattern, glue the shapes to a styrofoam block, and allow the stamp to dry overnight.

Step 3: Practice using the stamp. Press the track on the stamp pad and then on the paper.

Step 4: With a partner, create an animal track story on butcher paper. Stamp the animal tracks to show one of the following:
- one animal following another;
- place tracks farther apart to show an animal running;
- cluster the tracks in a small area to show that the animals found something to eat.

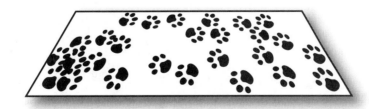

Criminal Mischief
Student Investigation

Crime Scene

As George Washington Carver Middle School students stepped off the bus, they were stunned to see the total destruction of their outdoor classroom. At first glance, it appeared as if someone had gone on a rampage. The Lewis and Clark wildflower plot had been trampled, plants in the butterfly garden had been ripped from the ground, the bird feeding station was in shambles, and mounds of soil from freshly dug holes dotted the vegetable garden.

The project had been controversial from the start. Many parents did not feel it was necessary to provide an outdoor, hands-on science education experience for the middle school students. People living near the school complained the facilities would be a magnet for wildlife. They believed the animals would eventually become a nuisance by snacking on flower beds and darting into traffic on busy streets. Pet owners feared the wildlife might carry diseases such as rabies or Lyme disease.

Students watched two police officers secure the area with yellow crime scene tape. The detectives and crime scene investigators arrived, put on plastic gloves, and walked through what was left of the outdoor classroom. They looked for a motive for the destruction. The only physical evidence found were animal tracks left in the vegetable garden area. The investigators took pictures and made sketches of the crime scene and the tracks. The detective felt the tracks were the key to solving the case. Who or what is responsible for the destruction of the outdoor classroom?

Suspect Information
1. Madison is a student at George Washington Carver Middle School. Last week, Madison was suspended from school for bullying another student during science class.
2. Jordan is a student at George Washington Carver Middle School. His two dogs, Shorty Boy and Shaggy Muffin, follow him everywhere.
3. Mrs. Martin, an elderly widow, lives across the street from the school with her small dog, Trixie Girl. She is opposed to the outdoor classroom. She fears it might attract wildlife carrying rabies.
4. Mr. Scott is the local animal control officer. His job is to enforce the city's leash law, pick up stray dogs and cats, and track and trap wildlife that have become a nuisance to residents of the city.

Investigation Directions
Criminal mischief plagues almost every community in the country. It presents special challenges for law enforcement and takes a variety of forms, from broken windows to graffiti to the total destruction of property.

Step 1: Read the Investigation Report page.
Step 2: Complete the Mammal Tracking Analysis Lab page.
Step 3: Use the information from your investigations to identify the prime suspect.

Investigation Report

Suspect Statements

People suspected of a crime are asked to give a statement. The statement often reveals the suspect's connection to the crime, where they were at the time of the crime, or a possible motive for committing the crime.

Madison: "In civics class, we learned that perpetrators of criminal mischief are typically middle-school boys. Living near the school makes our rose garden a good target for their malicious pranks. Since my mom got rid of the family cat and bought a guard dog, we haven't had any more trouble."

Jordan: "Shorty Boy and Shaggy Muffin are my two best friends. I rescued them from the animal shelter last year. If there are any more complaints about them disturbing the neighbors or digging in the outdoor classroom's butterfly garden, my parents plan to return the dogs to the shelter."

Mrs. Martin: "Kids have no respect for people's property nowadays. Those middle-school students have trampled my flower beds, trashed my yard, and frightened my poor dog, Trixie Girl, for the last time!"

Mr. Scott: "I have been called to this neighborhood on several occasions to track and trap skunks, raccoons, and opossums. I have warned the middle school biology teacher that the wild animals are attracted to the availability of food, water, and shelter provided by the outdoor classroom garden area. Removing the outdoor classroom would encourage these wild animals to leave the area and make my job easier."

Investigator's Notes

A detective locates and questions witnesses about suspicious activity in the area of the crime scene. They evaluate a witness's information and compare it with all the related data they have gathered.

Witness #1: "At night, it is like a wildlife preserve in this neighborhood. I noticed Mr. Scott leaving the school yard carrying his animal rescue bag and an animal cage last night. This is the third time this week I have seen the animal control van parked outside the school."

Witness #2: "I saw a kid with a backpack and two scruffy looking mutts cut across Mrs. Martin's yard last night. Mrs. Martin came out on her porch and yelled at the kid. He didn't even stop to see what she wanted, but kept on running toward the school yard."

Witness #3: "I was watching the sunset out my kitchen window last night. I saw Madison chasing her dog. He was chasing something small and furry across the middle-school parking lot. In my opinion, that girl and her dog are nothing but trouble."

Name: _____ Date: _____

Mammal Track Analysis Lab

Directions: Examine the four animal prints found at the crime scene. Use the information found on the Mammal Track Characteristics and Animal Tracking Guide pages to identify the mammal prints. Look for any identifiable features, such as print shape, the number of toes, and the presence or absence of claws. Record the information on the table. Analyze each of the prints to determine which match the prints from the crime scene.

Prints	Identifiable Features	Identify the Mammal

Whodunit?

Who is the prime suspect in the criminal mischief case? Use evidence and details from the investigation to support your conclusion.

_____

_____

_____

_____

Case #5
Break-In

Science Skills
classify
compare
predict
interpret data
draw inferences

Teacher Information

Crime Location: The middle-school science classroom is the crime scene.

Crime: Someone has broken into the science classroom.

Investigation: Students analyze soil samples to solve the crime.

Time Required: The student investigation takes approximately three 50-minute sessions to complete.

Materials Needed
- Skill-Building Activity pages and Student Investigation pages for each student
- See Soil and pH Analysis Lab pages for a list of materials needed for each lab

Teacher Notes

1. <u>Skill-Building Activity:</u> Guide students through the Soil Characteristics and Soil Lab activity pages. Provide 4 soil samples for students to use in the Soil Lab (example: lawn soil, potting soil, sandy soil, poor soil). Guide students through the Soil Lab page.
2. <u>Crime Scenario:</u> Students read and discuss the Break-In: Student Investigation page.
3. <u>Investigation:</u> Divide the class into teams. Instruct each team to read and discuss the information found on the Investigation Report page. Next, students complete the pH Analysis Lab page. Before the lab, collect 3 different types of soil (example: lawn soil, potting soil, sandy soil, poor soil). For each team, prepare five containers of soil. Label one container "crime scene evidence." Label the other containers with the names of the four suspects: Gage, Mikayla, Luis, and Alexis. Place the same type of soil in containers labeled Gage, Mikalya, and crime scene evidence. Place a different type of soil in each of the other containers.
4. <u>Solve the Crime:</u> Students use the evidence to identify the prime suspect. Teams present their conclusions. There isn't one "correct" answer. The cases are purposely designed to allow students to formulate different plausible solutions based on their interpretations of the evidence.

NSES Science as Inquiry: Content Standard A:
As a result of activities in grades 5–8, all students should develop abilities necessary to do scientific inquiry.

NSES Life Science: Content Standard D:
As a result of activities in grades 5–8, all students should develop an understanding of the structure of the earth system.

Resources
<http://school.discoveryeducation.com/schooladventures/soil/>
("The Dirt on Soil," Discovery Education)

Bial, Raymond. *A Handful of Dirt*. Walker and Company, 2000.

Soil Characteristics
Skill-Building Activity

Almost anyone who is present at a crime can affect the scene by picking up or leaving soil evidence behind. Since the early 1930s, the Federal Bureau of Investigation (FBI) has collected and studied soil for criminal investigations. Soil collected at a crime scene is examined at crime labs and is often used as physical evidence during crime trials.

Soil is a mixture of nonliving things, such as sand grains, smaller rock particles, and minerals. Soil also contains organic material that comes from decaying dead plants and animals. It also holds living things, both plants and animals. There are many different types of soil, and each one has unique characteristics. Forensic scientists examine the physical and chemical properties of soil collected at the crime scene. The results of their investigation can provide detectives with the information needed to help solve the crime.

Soil Characteristics

Characteristic	Description	Examples
Color: depends on the amount of air, water, organic matter, and certain elements in the soil	• Brown to black: accumulation of organic matter, humus • Purplish-black: accumulation of manganese • Yellow to reddish: accumulation of iron • White to gray: accumulation of salt	Scientists use the Munsell color system when describing soil samples.
Texture: determines how well water drains from a soil. Sands promote drainage better than clays.	• Sandy: feels rough • Silt: feels soft, silky, or floury • Clay: smooth when dry; sticky when wet	Rubbing soil samples between fingers can help identify the texture.

Soil Characteristics (cont.)

Characteristic	Description	Examples
Structure: the arrangement of smaller soil particles: sand, silt, and clay to form larger pieces	• Granular: individual particles of sand, silt and clay grouped together in small, round grains • Blocky: soil particles cling together in block shapes • Prismatic: soil particles have formed into vertical pillars • Platy: soil particles form thin sheets piled horizontally on one another	
Chemical Condition: influences what grows and lives in the soil	• Soil is measured by pH values of 1–14: • pH of 7 is neutral • pH below 7 is acidic • pH above 7 is alkaline	Litmus paper is used to test the pH levels of soil. pH Scale

Name: _____ Date: _____

Soil Lab
Skill-Building Activity

Purpose: identify characteristics of soil samples

Materials Needed: four types of soil (lawn soil, potting soil, sandy soil, poor soil)
magnifying glass   styrofoam cups   beaker   graduated cylinder   water   pencil

Soil Test #1-Color: Examine the soil samples, and record their color on the table below.

Sample #1	Sample #2	Sample #3	Sample #4

Soil Test #2-Composition: Examine soil samples using a magnifying glass. Identify any decaying plant or animal matter, debris, and/or living organisms found in the samples. Record the data on the table below.

Sample #1	Sample #2	Sample #3	Sample #4

Soil Test #3-Texture: Rub each soil sample between your fingers. Identify the texture, and record the data on the table below.

Sample #1	Sample #2	Sample #3	Sample #4

Soil Test #4-Water-Holding Capacity: Using a pencil, punch a small hole in the bottom of a styrofoam cup. Add soil until the cup is half full. Hold the cup over a beaker. Add 100 mL of water to the graduated cylinder. Then, pour water over the top of the soil. On the table below, record the amount of time it takes the water to collect in the beaker.

Sample #1	Sample #2	Sample #3	Sample #4

Break-In
Student Investigation

Crime Scene

On Tuesday morning, Mrs. Garcia walked to her classroom hoping to finish printing the computer-generated progress reports for her science students. As she entered the room, Mrs. Garcia frowned. A window was left open overnight. Mrs. Garcia was alarmed to find a trail of dirt leading from the row of seats near the window to her desk. She quickly sat down at her computer. The grade book program she was using on Monday was open. Mrs. Garcia checked each class report. She was stunned to find the grades for her 7th hour students were missing.

Mrs. Garcia contacted the principal, who decided to turn the matter over to the police. Investigators determined the perpetrator entered and exited the classroom through the open window. The soil was collected using a portable vacuum cleaner equipped with a paper filter. The filter was bagged and sent to the forensic lab.

Mrs. Garcia was interviewed by a detective. She gave him the names of four students in her 7th hour class that sat near the open window. Soil samples were taken from the shoes of each student. The students had a motive: grades were used to determine eligibility for middle-school sponsored activities. Who was responsible for the break-in?

Suspect Information

1. Gage is a member of the Green Thumb Club. Club members do the landscaping work around the building after school and/or on the weekends.
2. Mikayla is a member of the Entrepreneur Club. The members are responsible for operating the school store, Shop n' Go. They sell snacks and school supplies.
3. Zackary is a member of the Environmental Club. Members meet one or two times per month. Activities include maintaining the middle-school recycling program and organizing the school's Earth Day activities.
4. Selena is a member of the Golf Pro Club. Members practice at the Briar Creek Golf Course on weekends.

Investigation Directions

School break-ins pose a serious problem for schools, communities, and the police and fire departments charged with protecting them. Those who break into schools are typically middle school students (roughly 12–15 years-old).

Step 1:   Read the Investigation Report page.
Step 2:   Complete the pH Analysis Lab.
Step 3:   Use the evidence from your investigation to identify the prime suspect.

Investigation Report

Suspect Statements

People suspected of a crime are asked to give a statement. The statement often reveals the suspect's connection with the crime, where they were at the time of the crime, and a possible motive for committing the crime.

Gage: "I don't like Mrs. Garcia, and she doesn't like me. She is mean, grouchy, and rude. She only calls on me when I don't know the answer. I told my parents she is always telling me to sit down and be quiet."

Mikayla: "You've probably seen my name in the newspaper. My poem won first place at the Language Arts Fair, I was student of the month for December, and I am president of the Entrepreneurs Club. I have never had a missing assignment until I had Mrs. Garcia for a teacher. She will not give anyone a break."

Zackary: "I love science. Mrs. Garcia is my favorite teacher. We are always doing hands-on activities that help us understand the science we read about in our textbook. Even so, science is hard for me. If I don't get my science grade up to passing, I will have to drop out of the Environmental Club."

Selena: "My parents will not accept poor grades. If I do not make all A's, I will be grounded. Mrs. Garcia has been tutoring me after school, and my grades have improved. I don't think I will get an A in her class, though."

Investigator's Notes

Every crime has a criminal, and if the criminal is not identified immediately, then investigators look for evidence that might point to suspects. It is the job of the detectives to question these suspects. Suspects are asked to provide the detectives with an alibi: proof of their location at the time a crime is committed.

Gage: "After school, I helped the Green Thumb Club plant poppy seeds around the school's flag pole for our annual Memorial Day celebration. We worked until dark. I walked home afterwards."

Mikayla: "The Entrepreneur Club had a meeting after school. At 4:30 P.M., I stopped to talk to Gage while he planted poppy seeds. Then, I met Selena. We walked part of the way home together. Selena had forgotten her golf bag and went back to school to get it."

Zackary: "Monday from 4:00 to 7:00 P.M. I helped the Environmental Club stack the newspapers we had collected in the recycling bin. My parents picked me up at 7:30 P.M."

Selena: "Mrs. Garcia tutors me after school on Mondays from 3:30 to 4:30. I saw Zackary helping stack newspapers in the recycling bins on my way to the Briar Creek Golf Course."

Name: _____ Date: _____

pH Analysis Lab

Soil evidence can be a valuable clue in linking the crime scene to a suspect. One way to find similarities in the soil evidence is to compare the pH of each sample.

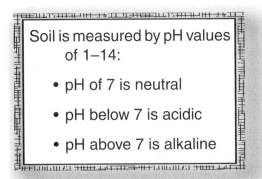

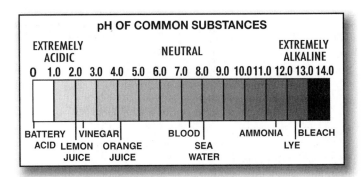

Purpose: Compare pH levels of the soil found at the crime scene to soil found on the shoes of each suspect.

Materials Needed: styrofoam cup   glass stirring rod   pH chart
                      litmus paper   filter paper   water

Directions:
Step 1: Place a small sample of each suspect's soil sample in a Styrofoam cup. Label each cup.
Step 2: Add 100 mL of water to each cup and stir.
Step 3: Pour the water and soil through a funnel lined with filter paper. Collect the water in a glass beaker and label it. Throw away the used filter and reline the funnel with a clean filter. Repeat the steps for each sample.
Step 4: Using litmus paper, check the pH of each water sample. Record the data on the table below.

pH Level of Soil Samples

Crime Scene	Gage's Shoe	Mikayla's Shoe	Zackary's Shoe	Selena's Shoe

Whodunit?

Who is the prime suspect in the break-in case? Use evidence and details from the investigation to support your conclusion.

_____

_____

_____

Case #6
Burglary

Science Skills
classify
compare
predict
interpret data
draw inferences

Teacher Information

Crime Location: The middle-school media center is the crime scene.

Crime: Someone stole the book fair money.

Investigation: Students compare the similarities and differences in DNA samples.

Time Required: The student investigation takes approximately two 50-minute sessions to complete.

Materials Needed
- Skill-Building Activity pages and Student Investigation pages for each student
- See the DNA Extraction Lab page for a list of materials needed for the lab

Teacher Notes
1. Skill-Building Activity: Guide students through the DNA Fingerprint and DNA Extraction Lab activity pages. (Students may have to experiment with the measurement amounts to see which work best when doing the lab.)
2. Crime Scenario: Students read and discuss the Crime Scene, Suspect Information, and Investigation Directions found on the Burglary: Student Investigation page.
3. Investigation: Divide the class into teams. Instruct each team to read and discuss the information found on the Investigation Report page. Next, students compare the DNA profile of the crime scene evidence to the DNA profiles of each of the suspects found on the DNA Analysis Lab page.
4. Solve the Crime: Students use the evidence to identify the prime suspect. Teams present their conclusions. There isn't one "correct" answer. The cases are purposely designed to allow students to formulate different plausible solutions based on their interpretations of the evidence.

NSES Science as Inquiry: Content Standard A:
As a result of activities in grades 5–8, all students should develop abilities necessary to do scientific inquiry.

NSES Life Science: Content Standard C:
As a result of activities in grades 5–8, all students should develop an understanding of reproduction and heredity.

Resources
<http://www.pbs.org/wgbh/nova/sheppard/analyze.html>
    ("Create a DNA Fingerprint," Public Broadcasting Service)

Fridell, Ron. *DNA: Fingerprinting.* Scholastic, Inc., 2001.

DNA Fingerprinting
Skill-Building Activity

DNA "fingerprinting" is a powerful tool that forensic scientists can use in criminal investigations. DNA is the material inside a cell that carries the genetic blueprint, the code of inherited characteristics. Everyone's DNA pattern is different, except for identical twins.

DNA is found in the chromosomes. Genes are sections of the chromosomes that determine certain traits, such as eye color, freckles, or dimples. Every living thing is a collection of these inherited traits. DNA from the parents is passed on to their offspring and combined to make a new set of chromosomes.

The nucleus of each cell holds the long strands of DNA. The scientific name for DNA is deoxyribonucleic acid. A single DNA strand looks like a long, spiraling ladder known as

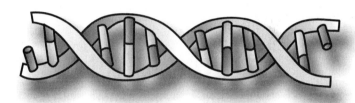

a double helix. There are thousands of rungs, or steps, on the ladder. The rungs are made up of four bases or chemicals: guanine, cytosine, thymine, and adenine. The order in which these bases are arranged on a strand of DNA is unique to every person. The number of steps and how they are arranged form a genetic code or pattern. This makes DNA fingerprinting a very effective tool for the identification of a criminal.

DNA fingerprinting is sometimes called DNA profiling. It allows the police to identify an individual in the same way as fingerprints do. In a forensic investigation, the genetic material is extracted from a suspect and analyzed. DNA samples can be taken from body fluids or almost any tissue, including hair, blood, saliva, or torn skin. The DNA pattern of a suspect and the crime scene evidence can now be compared to prove a suspect's innocence or guilt.

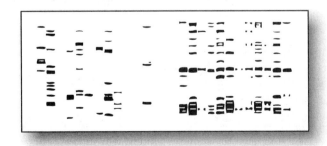

DNA fingerprints resemble bar codes found on packaging labels.

Name: _____ Date: _____

DNA Extraction Lab
Skill-Building Activity

Purpose: extract DNA

Materials Needed
- 30 mL liquid dish soap
- $\frac{1}{8}$ teaspoon meat tenderizer
- 2 small beakers or jars
- 1 cup chopped onion

- toothpicks
- 30 mL warm water
- 1 teaspoon salt
- rubbing alcohol

- blender
- microscope
- slides
- funnel

* You may have to experiment with the measurement amounts to see what works best.

Procedure

Step 1: Blend together chopped onions, warm water, and salt for 5–10 seconds. Do not totally liquefy. Pour the mixture through a strainer into a clear glass beaker.

Step 2: Add liquid dish soap to the liquid in the glass beaker and mix gently with a toothpick for 3–5 minutes. Do not make bubbles.

Step 3: Add meat tenderizer to the liquid. Stir gently.

Step 4: Add the rubbing alcohol to the mixture. Slowly pour it down the side of the beaker so the alcohol forms a separate layer on top of the onion mixture. Pour until you have the same amount of alcohol in the beaker as the onion mixture.

Step 5: The clear, gooey strings floating to the top are DNA. The strands may have small bubbles attached to them. Slowly twist a strand onto a toothpick. (Do not scoop up scum from below the alcohol layer.

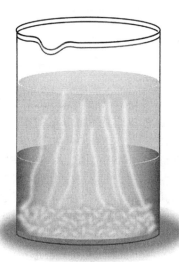

Observation

Observe the DNA under a microscope. Record your observations.

_____

_____

_____

_____

Burglary
Student Investigation

Crime Scene

Saturday morning about 150 people, a mix of parents, grandparents, and students, attended the middle-school book fair. Student volunteers played a big role in the success of the program. They assisted shoppers and acted as cashiers. At 5:00 P.M., Mrs. Allen, the media center specialist, closed the book fair, declaring the fund-raising event a great success.

Mrs. Allen counted the money in the cash register while student volunteers straightened book supples, cleaned up the floors, and emptied trash cans. She thanked all the volunteers as they left to go home. Mrs. Allen grabbed her purse, locked the doors, and followed the last student out of the school.

Mrs. Allen returned to school a few minutes later with a hamburger and a soft drink. She planned to finish the book fair paperwork and fill out the bank deposit slip. Approaching the media center, she was alarmed to see a broken window pane in the entry door. She immediately left the building and called the police department on her cell phone.

Two officers responded to the call. After speaking briefly with Mrs. Allen, they entered the school. The officers found the book fair cash register drawer open and the money missing. Several used tissues were found on the floor near the empty cash register. The tissues were bagged and taken to the crime lab for DNA profiling.

Mrs. Allen was interviewed by a detective. She gave him the names of four middle-school students whom she felt had an opportunity and a motive to steal the book fair money. Who is responsible for the burglary?

Suspect Information
1. Anthony worked as a student volunteer at the book fair. He was in charge of the poster and sticker counter.
2. Daniel attended the book fair on Saturday. He caused a disturbance, and Mrs. Allen asked him to leave.
3. Breanne and Brittany are identical twins. Breanne did not attend the book fair Saturday. She didn't have any money to spend on a book, and she had the sniffles. Brittany was a student volunteer. Her job was to bag each customer's purchases.

Investigation Directions
When a person illegally enters a home, business, or school with the intent to steal, they are committing a burglary. These criminals often unknowingly leave evidence behind, such as body fluids or tissues, which can connect them to the crime.

Step 1: Read the Investigation Report page.
Step 2: Complete the DNA Analysis Lab page.
Step 3: Use the evidence from your investigation to identify the prime suspect.

Investigation Report

Suspect Statements

People suspected of a crime are asked to give a statement. The statement often reveals the suspect's connection with the crime, where they were at the time of the crime, and a possible motive for committing the crime.

Anthony: "On Saturday, I was in charge of the poster and sticker counter. I really wanted to buy the dog poster, but I didn't have any money. I had lost two library books, and my parents made me pay for them with my book fair money."

Breanne: "I didn't attend the book fair on Saturday. My text messaging racked up a huge cell phone bill. My parents made me use my allowance to help pay the bill."

Brittany: "My job as a volunteer was to bag each customer's purchases. There were several books I really wanted to buy, but I am saving my money for volleyball camp. If I don't have the money saved by this spring, my parents said I wouldn't be able to attend."

Daniel: "I wanted one of the skull key chains, but everything was too expensive. All I did was complain about the price. Mrs. Allen said I was causing a disturbance and kicked me out."

Investigator's Notes

Every crime has a criminal, and if the criminal is not identified immediately, then investigators look for evidence that might point to suspects. It is the job of the detectives to question these suspects. Suspects are asked to provide the detectives with an alibi: proof of their location at the time a crime is committed.

Anthony: "I left the book fair early because I forgot to take my allergy medicine, and I couldn't stop sneezing. I told Mrs. Allen goodbye, and then I rode my bike home. I saw Daniel and some other skateboarders at the park near my house."

Breanne: "After the book fair, I met Brittany outside the school. We walked to the public library to work on our social studies project. I went to the computer room to type our report. Our parents picked us up at 8:00 P.M. Saturday evening."

Brittany: "After the book fair closed, Mrs. Allen asked me to pick up any paper on the floor and empty the garbage cans. When I finished my job, I met my sister outside the school, and we walked to the public library. While Breanne typed our report, I checked out several books."

Daniel: "I left the book fair and met some friends at the park. I went home about dark. I saw Anthony, Mrs. Allen's favorite student, riding his bike."

Name: _____ Date: _____

DNA Analysis Lab

Directions: DNA fingerprinting is sometimes called DNA profiling. It allows the police to identify an individual in the same way as fingerprints do. Analyze each of the DNA samples to determine which suspect's DNA matches the DNA from the crime scene.

Crime Scene DNA	Suspect #1 Anthony	Suspect #2 Breanne	Suspect #3 Daniel	Suspect #4 Brittany

Whodunit?

Who is the prime suspect in the burglary case? Use evidence and details from the investigation to support your conclusion.

_____

_____

_____

_____

Case #7
Petty Larceny

Science Skills
classify
compare
predict
interpret data
draw inferences

Teacher Information
Crime Location: The middle-school teacher's workroom is the crime scene.

Crime: Someone stole money from the soda machine.

Investigation: Students use paper chromatography to separate dyes found in different brands of lipstick.

Time Required: The student investigation takes approximately two 50-minute sessions to complete.

Materials Needed
- Skill-Building Activity pages and Student Investigation pages for each student
- See the Chromatography Lab and Lipstick Chromatography Lab pages for a list of materials needed for the lab. (Make sure the lipsticks for the lab are soluble in acetone.)

Teacher Notes
1. <u>Skill-Building Activity:</u> Guide students through the Chromatography Lab activity pages.
2. <u>Crime Scenario:</u> Students read and discuss the Crime Scene, Suspect Information, and Investigation Directions found on the Petty Larceny Student Investigation page.
3. <u>Investigation:</u> Divide the class into teams. Instruct each team to read and discuss the information found on the Investigation Report page. Next, students complete the Lipstick Analysis Lab and Lipstick Chromatography Data Sheet pages. (The lab requires the teacher to provide students with four different brands of acetone-soluble red lipstick. Label each tube with a suspect's name. Prepare the two cola cans found at the crime scene. Label the cans: Cola Can #1 and Cola Can #2. Apply one of the suspect's lipsticks to your lips, then place your lips on the drinking area of the can. Clean your lips. Using another suspect's lipstick, repeat the process on the other can.)
4. <u>Solve the Crime:</u> Students use the evidence to identify the prime suspect. Teams present their conclusions. There isn't one "correct" answer. The cases are purposely designed to allow students to formulate different plausible solutions based on their interpretations of the evidence.

NSES Science as Inquiry: Content Standard A:
As a result of activities in grades 5–8, all students should develop abilities necessary to do scientific inquiry.

NSES Science as Inquiry: Content Standard B:
As a result of activities in grades 5–8, all students should develop an understanding of the properties and changes of properties in matter.

Resources
<http://www.accessexcellence.org/LC/SS/chromatography_background.html>
("An Introduction to Chromatography," The National Health Museum)

Campbell, Andrea. *Detective Notebook: Crime Scene Science.* Sterling Publishing, 2004.

Chromatography Lab
Skill-Building Activity

Forensic scientists can identify all sorts of substances left behind at a crime scene using one of the many types of chromatography. In paper chromatography, a small amount of the substance to be analyzed is placed on a strip of paper. The paper is placed in a solvent, a liquid that can dissolve the substance. The paper absorbs the solvent. As the chemicals in the substance are dissolved, they travel at different speeds up the paper, forming a colored pattern on the paper. The pattern created is like a fingerprint. It can be used by investigators to identify the original substance.

Purpose: observe the process of chromatography

Materials Needed:
white paper towels
colored water-soluble
    markers: black, red,
    green, yellow, blue,
    orange, brown
solvent (water)
glass beaker
pencil
clear tape
scissors
ruler
plastic or foam plate

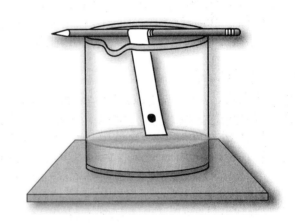

Procedure:

Step 1: Pour 30 mL of solvent into the glass beaker.
Step 2: Cut the paper towel into six 2 cm x 10 cm strips.
Step 3: Tape a strip to the pencil.
Step 4: With the black marker, place a dot 2 cm from one end of the paper towel strip.
Step 5: Lay the pencil across the rim of the glass beaker. Adjust the length of the paper towel so it just touches the solvent when placed in the beaker.
Step 6: Observe what happens as the water moves through the dot.
Step 7: Remove the strip and place it on a plate to dry.
Step 8: Repeat steps 1–7 for the red, green, yellow, blue, and orange colored markers.
Step 9: Tape the dried paper strips to the table found on the Paper Chromatography Data Sheet page.

Name: _____ Date: _____

Chromatography Data Sheet
Skill-Building Activity

Directions: Tape the paper towel strips to the correct column on the data table below. Count and record the number of dye colors used to create the original marker color.

Black	Red	Green	Yellow	Blue	Orange
Total # of dye colors _____	Total # of dye colors _____	Total # of dye colors _____	Total # of dye colors _____	Total # of dye colors _____	Total # of dye colors _____

Predict the number of colors needed to create a brown color. _____

Repeat the lab using a brown marker. How many colors did you discover were used to create

the brown color? _____

Explain how paper chromatography could be used to solve a crime. _____

_____

_____

Petty Larceny
Student Investigation

Crime Scene

As the performers danced and spun across the illuminated stage, ushers led people to their seats. Some performers sang as they leapt into the air, while others tipped their pirate hats and marched in place. Swords clashed as Peter Pan and Captain Hook battled across the stage for Never Never Land. Behind the curtain, the stagehands whispered into headsets and prepared actors for the upcoming scene. The audience found it hard to believe the performers were only seventh- and eighth-grade students. From the choreographed scenes to the fitted costumes, the show had the feel of a Broadway theatre production. The thunderous applause as the curtain closed on the last act signaled the success of the production. The hours of hard work and dedication by the Monroe Middle School Drama Class had paid off.

The performers took their final bow and rushed off stage. The applause, laughter, and congratulations echoed in the halls. The cast and crew headed for the dressing rooms, ready to celebrate their success. On the way, they saw two police officers talking quietly to the principal, Mrs. Conrad. Soon rumors began to circulate that someone had pried open the soda machine in the teacher's workroom. About $75 in cash had been taken. The crime had been committed that evening, sometime during the performance. The only evidence collected by investigators was two cola cans with lipstick prints on the rims.

The police interviewed the drama teacher, Mr. Smith. Investigators learned that several students had an opportunity to commit the crime. Later, four students were questioned by detectives. Who will be charged with petty larceny?

Suspect Information

1. Dominic played Captain Hook in the production of *Peter Pan*.
2. Tamika was the producer of the play.
3. Carlie was an usher for the evening performance of the play.
4. Levi played Peter Pan in the production of *Peter Pan*.

Investigation Directions

Stealing is taking something without permission. This is illegal. Petty larceny is a crime involving the theft of something valued at less than $250. Evidence left behind by a thief can be used to determine the innocence or guilt of those accused and to help solve the crime.

Step 1: Read the Investigation Report page.

Step 2: Complete the Lipstick Analysis Lab page and the Lipstick Chromatography Data Sheet page.

Step 3: Use the evidence from your investigation to identify the prime suspect.

Investigation Report

Suspect Statements

People suspected of a crime are asked to give a statement. The statement often reveals the suspect's connection with the crime, where they were at the time of the crime, and a possible motive for committing the crime.

Dominic: "Both the male and female actors were trained in basic stage makeup techniques to enhance our natural features and change our appearance."

Tamika: "As the producer, it was my job to make sure all the actors in the play had their own makeup kits. They were told to keep their cosmetic tools and makeup organized in a small toolbox or tackle box."

Carlie: "My job included passing out programs, answering questions about performance times, and reminding patrons to turn off cell phones and beepers during the performance."

Levi: "My role as Peter Pan required me to wear makeup. Mr. Smith asked all the actors to add color to our cheeks and lips because the stage lights tended to wash out our faces."

Investigator's Notes

A detective locates and questions witnesses about persons seen or believed to have been in the area at the time of the crime. Observations, descriptions, and identifications made by witnesses can be useful in solving a crime. Investigators evaluate a witness's information and compare it with the related data they have gathered.

Witness #1 Mr. Smith: "All the actors are required to use foundation, lipstick, and eye shadow to enhance or change their appearance. Several of the boys were opposed to wearing the stage makeup."

Witness #2 Stagehand: "Before the play, Tamika had each actor stand under the stage lights to see how their makeup looked from the back row of the gym. There was an argument between Tamika and Levi because he refused to wear the lipstick."

Witness #3 Usher: "Carlie and I were ushers. Our job was to pass out programs and seat people as they entered the auditorium. Halfway through the first act, Carlie disappeared. I found her in the restroom drinking a cola and applying makeup."

Witness #4 Janitor: "The teacher's workroom was left open for the cast and crew of the play to use. I saw Dominic and Tamika drinking a cola and talking during intermission in the room. Dominic was carrying his makeup kit."

Lipstick Analysis Lab

A lipstick smear left at the scene of a crime can be a valuable piece of trace evidence. You will use a technique known as paper chromatography to distinguish among the brands of lipstick used by each of the suspects and compare them to the lipstick found at the crime scene.

In paper chromatography, a small amount of the lipstick to be analyzed is placed on a strip of paper. The paper is placed in a solvent. As the chemicals in the lipstick are dissolved by the solvent, they travel at different speeds up the paper, forming a colored pattern. The pattern can be used by investigators to identify the suspect who left behind the trace evidence of lipstick at the crime scene.

Purpose: compare lipstick samples using paper chromatography

Materials Needed:
6 chromatographypaperstrips
4 tubes of acetone-soluble
   red lipstick (each labeled
   with a suspect's name)
2 cola cans with lipstick on
   rim (labeled #1 and #2)
solvent (acetone)
6 glass beakers
6 pencils
clear tape
scissors
ruler
plastic or foam plate

Step 1: Pour 30 mL of solvent into each beaker.

Step 2: Place a pencil line 2 cm from the end of each chromatography paper strip.

Step 3: Using cola can #1, smear a sample of the lipstick from the can's rim onto the paper strip at the pencil line. Repeat the procedure for can #2.

Step 4: Using one of the suspect's lipsticks, place a dot on a paper strip at the pencil line. Repeat the procedure for each of the other suspects' lipsticks with separate strips of paper.

Step 5: Tape each strip to a pencil. Adjust the length of the paper towel so it just touches the solvent when placed in the beaker.

Step 6: Lay the pencil across the rim of the glass beaker, dipping the paper in the solvent.

Step 7: Remove each strip from the solvent and place it on a plate to dry.

Step 8: Tape the dried paper strips to the table found on the Lipstick Chromatography Data Sheet page.

Name: _____ Date: _____

Lipstick Chromatography Data Sheet

Directions: Tape the dry paper strips to the data table below. Examine the lipstick chromatography results. Analyze all the color patterns to determine which suspect's lipstick matches the lipstick from the crime scene.

Cola Can #1	Cola Can #2	Suspect #1 Dominic	Suspect #2 Tamika	Suspect #3 Carlie	Suspect #4 Levi

Whodunit?

Who is the prime suspect in the petty larceny case? Use evidence and details from the investigation to support your conclusion.

_____

_____

_____

_____

Case #8
Arson

Teacher Information

Crime Location: The middle-school supply closet is the crime scene.

Crime: Someone set a fire.

Investigation: Students compare the bite mark evidence from the crime scene to the bite mark impressions of the suspects.

Time Required: The student investigation takes approximately two 50-minute sessions to complete.

Materials Needed

- Skill-Building Activity pages and Student Investigation pages for each student
- See the Bite Mark Lab page for a list of materials needed for the lab

Teacher Notes

1. Skill-Building Activity: Guide students through the Forensic Dentistry and Teeth Impression Lab activity pages.

2. Crime Scenario: Students read and discuss the Crime Scene, Suspect Information, and Investigation Directions found on the Arson Student Investigation page.

3. Investigation: Divide the class into teams. Instruct each team to read and discuss the information found on the Investigation Report page. Next, students compare the crime scene evidence to the bite mark impressions of each suspect found on the Bite Mark Analysis Lab page. The lab requires the teacher to provide each team with five different sets of bite mark impression plates. Two sets of the plates should be made by the same person. Label one set 'evidence' and the other 'Suspect #3: Matthew.' For the lab, use only Matthew's top impression plate. Bite mark evidence rarely includes a full set of teeth. Label the remaining three plates 'Suspect #1: Samantha,' 'Suspect #2: Andrew,' and 'Suspect #4: Hannah.'

4. Solve the Crime: Students use the evidence to identify the prime suspect. Teams present their conclusions. The cases are purposely designed to allow students to formulate different plausible solutions based on their interpretations of the evidence.

NSES Science as Inquiry: Content Standard A:
As a result of activities in grades 5–8, all students should develop abilities necessary to do scientific inquiry.

Resources

<http://www.forensicdentistryonline.org/Forensic_pages_1/bitemarkguide.htm>
("On-line study guides-Bitemarks," Forensic Dental Services)

Watts, Franklin. *The Right Bite.* Scholastic Library Publishing, 2006.

Forensic Dentistry
Skill-Building Activity

Sometimes bite marks can be helpful in connecting a suspect to a crime. Teeth are like tools. They can leave identifiable marks on certain objects: pencils, food, chewing gum, or even on the skin. The pattern of the teeth (shape, size, number of teeth) is different for every person, even identical twins. Children have sharper teeth than adults because over time, chewing gradually wears down the surface of the teeth. Some people have chipped or missing teeth. Since everyone's teeth are different, people can be identified by their bite marks. A forensic dentist or odontologist looks for points of similarity between a suspect's teeth impressions and the bite marks found at the scene of the crime.

Types of Teeth

People have two sets of teeth during their lifetimes. Children have 20 baby or primary teeth. By the age of 13, most teenagers have lost their primary teeth and have a full set of permanent teeth. The average adult has 32 permanent teeth.

A person's teeth are different shapes and sizes because each tooth has a special function.
- Canines are shaped for tearing food.
- Molars are shaped for grinding food.
- Premolars are shaped for cutting food.
- Incisors are shaped for biting food.

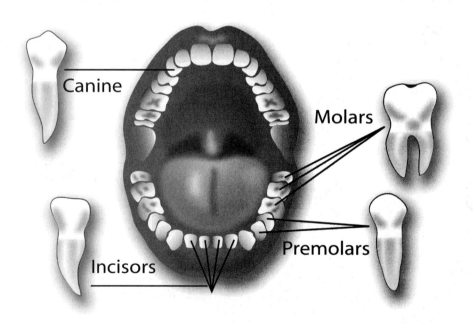

Name: _____ Date: _____

Teeth Impression Lab
Skill-Building Activity

Purpose: identify characteristics of bite marks

Materials Needed:
styrofoam plate
sanitary wipes
scissors
ink pen

Procedure:

Step 1: Cut two 6 cm by 8 cm rectangles from a styrofoam plate.

Step 2: Stack the two rectangular plates together and place the narrow end in your mouth as far as possible.

Step 3: Bite down firmly on the plates and them remove.

Step 4: Clean the teeth impressions with a sanitary wipe and let dry.

Step 5: Correctly label the set of plates "upper teeth" and "lower teeth."

Step 6: Examine your set of impressions. Compete the table below by placing an X on any tooth with a unique feature. Identify the tooth as incisor, canine, premolar, or molar, and describe the characteristics of the tooth (chipped, worn, misshapen, and/or missing). On the data table, record the information in the section labeled Upper and Lower teeth.

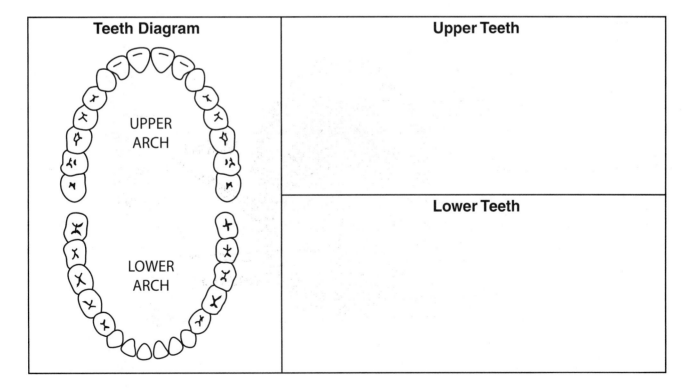

Teeth Diagram	Upper Teeth
UPPER ARCH / LOWER ARCH	
	Lower Teeth

Arson
Student Investigation

Crime Scene

At 2:30 P.M., Lane County Sheriff's deputies were dispatched to assist the Jordan Valley Fire and Rescue with a reported fire at the Harrison Middle School. A student entering the math room reported smelling smoke in the hallway. The fire alarm went off and students and staff evacuated the school. A blaze was discovered by the math teacher and a security guard; both helped to extinguish the fire. The building suffered only minor damages and no one was injured.

Based on where the fire started and evidence found at the scene, the investigator quickly suspected that the fire had been intentionally set. Trash had been piled in front of a storage closet that contained the recently completed TAP test booklets, the state-mandated exam for middle-school students. Several gum wrappers, a partially eaten candy bar, and a blue lighter were found a few feet from where the fire started. When the candy bar was examined, the forensic dentist found several teeth marks.

The damage from the fire forced school administrators to shuffle classroom assignments for the 610 students. At a press conference, Mrs. McDowell, principal of Harrison Middle School, said cleanup efforts would begin immediately. She told reporters that the fire had been started by an unknown person, but the police did have suspects: four students who attended the middle school. Investigators took impressions of each suspect's teeth. They compared bite marks left on the candy bar to each suspect's bite mark impressions. Who is guilty of arson?

Suspect Information

1. Samantha was suspended from school for smoking in the restroom.
2. Andrew set a fire in a restroom during lunch hour in third grade. The school was evacuated, and one student was treated for smoke inhalation.
3. Matthew has a history of playing with matches.
4. Hannah is the student who reported smelling smoke in the hall.

Investigation Directions

Arson is setting a fire with the purpose of destroying property. Students who set fires at school or on school grounds threaten the safety of other students and the school staff. An arsonist often leaves evidence behind at the crime scene. This evidence can be analyzed and used by investigators to help solve the crime.

Step 1: Read the Investigation Report page.
Step 2: Complete the Bite Mark Analysis Lab page.
Step 3: Use the evidence from your investigation to identify the prime suspect.

Investigation Report

Suspect Statements

People suspected of a crime are asked to give a statement. The statement often reveals the suspect's connection with the crime, where they were at the time of the crime, and a possible motive for committing the crime.

Samantha: "Some of my friends talked me into smoking my first cigarette in sixth grade. I thought it was cool. Once you start smoking, it is hard to stop, especially if everyone around you is smoking and offering you cigarettes."

Andrew: "In third grade, I found a lighter on the way to school. I was messing with it in the boys' restroom and accidentally set the paper in the trash can on fire."

Matthew: "I got into a lot of trouble last year over a dumb prank. I was playing basketball with my friends at the park. They dared me to set the trash in the garbage can on fire."

Hannah: "The tardy bell had rung, and I was hurrying to class. I smelled smoke. When I got to class, I reported it to the teacher."

Investigator's Notes

A detective locates and questions witnesses about persons seen or believed to have been in the area at the time of the crime. Observations, descriptions, and identifications made by witnesses can be useful in solving a crime. Investigators evaluate a witness's information and compare it with the related data they have gathered.

Witness #1 Seventh-Grade Student: "I overheard Matthew and Samantha talking in the lunch line about the TAP test. They were being very secretive. When Samantha noticed me listening, she got in my face, smacked her gum loudly, and told me to mind my own business."

Witness #2 School Secretary: "Andrew entered my office just after the 7th hour bell rang. He had been caught by the math teacher sticking a wad of chewing gum under his desk."

Witness #3 Math Teacher: "The 7th hour tardy bell rang at 2:15. Hannah, who has been warned about being late to math class several times this term, came running down the hall a few minutes later. She ran into the room and caused a panic by screaming that the school was on fire."

Name: _____ Date: _____

Bite Mark Analysis Lab

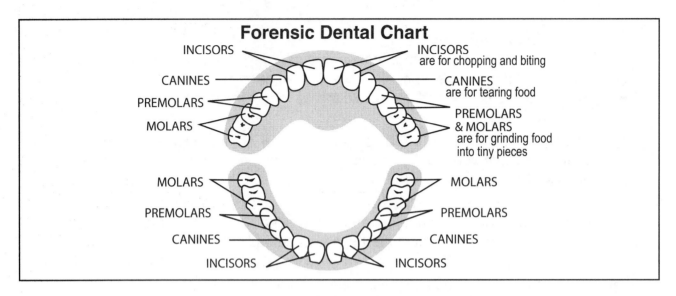

Directions: Using the Forensic Dental Chart, complete the table below by placing an X on any tooth with a unique feature. Identify the tooth as incisor, canine, premolar, or molar, and describe the characteristics of the tooth (chipped, worn, misshapen, and/or missing). On the data table, record the information in the section labeled Upper and Lower teeth. Analyze each of the impressions to determine which matches the evidence from the crime scene.

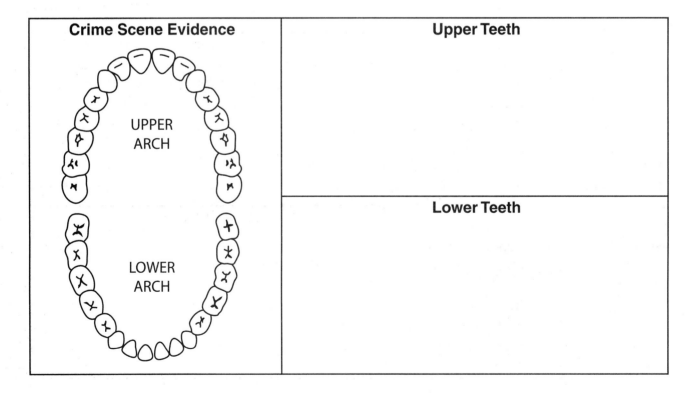

Name: _____ Date: _____

Teeth Impressions of the Suspects

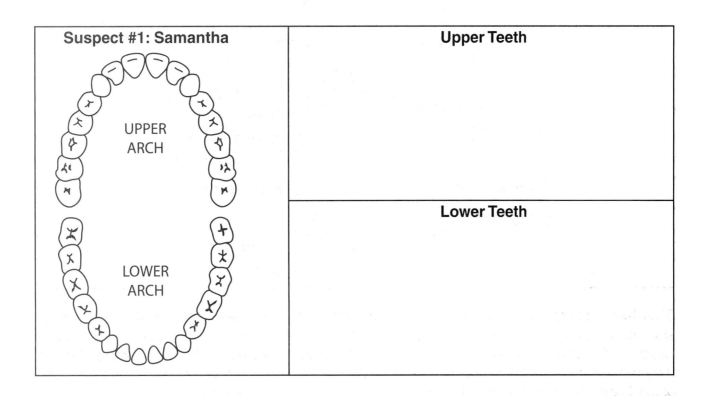

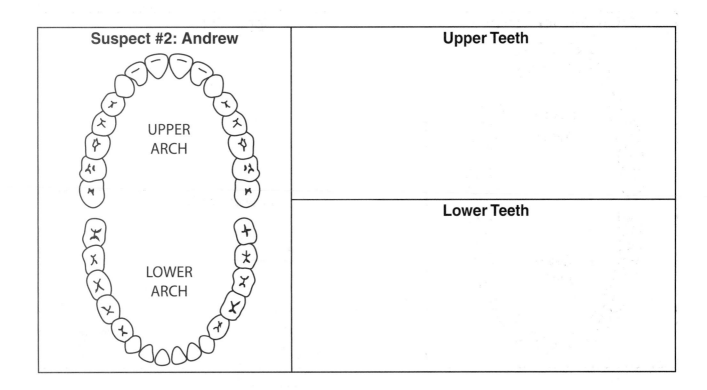

Name: _____ Date: _____

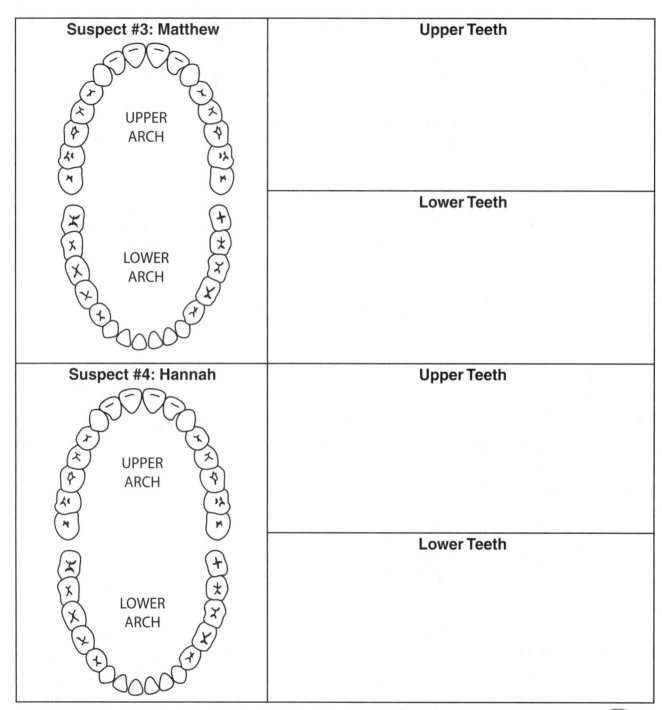

Suspect #3: Matthew	Upper Teeth
	Lower Teeth
Suspect #4: Hannah	Upper Teeth
	Lower Teeth

Whodunit?

Who is the prime suspect in the arson case? Use evidence and details from the investigation to support your conclusion.

_____

_____

_____

Case #9
Vandalism

Science Skills
classify
compare
predict
interpret data
draw inferences

Teacher Information
Crime Location: The middle-school bus parking lot is the crime scene.
Crime: Someone vandalized the school's fleet of buses.
Investigation: Students compare shoe prints.
Time Required: The student investigation takes approximately three 50-minute sessions to complete.

Materials Needed
- Skill-Building Activity pages and Student Investigation pages for each student
- See the Patent Print Lab and Shoe Print Analysis Lab pages for a list of materials needed for the lab (Provide students with a variety of old shoes to use in the labs).

Teacher Notes
1. <u>Skill-Building Activity:</u> Guide students through the Patent Print Lab and Shoe Print Analysis Lab activity pages.
2. <u>Crime Scenario:</u> Students read and discuss the Crime Scene, Suspect Information, and Investigation Directions found on the Vandalism: Student Investigation page.
3. <u>Investigation:</u> Divide the class into teams. Instruct each team to read and discuss the information found on the Investigation Report page. Next, students compare the Shoe Print Analysis Lab and the Shoe Print Data Sheet pages. (The lab requires the teacher to collect four different sports shoes. Two shoes should have a similar tread. The morning of the activity, dampen the ground where the activity will occur. Select two of the shoes and make as many sets of shoe prints in the mud as there are teams. The prints should be about 1 cm deep. After making the prints, clean the shoes to use in the lab. Label on shoes Suspect #1: Alex and the other Suspect #4: Sabrina. Each team will make a cast of each shoe print to use in the lab.)
4. <u>Solve the Crime:</u> Students use the evidence to identify the prime suspect. Teams present their conclusions. There isn't one "correct" answer. The cases are purposely designed to allow students to formulate different plausible solutions based on their interpretations of the evidence.

NSES Science as Inquiry: Content Standard A:
As a result of activities in grades 5–8, all students should develop abilities necessary to do scientific inquiry.

Resources
<http://www.ojp.usdoj.gov/nij/journals/258/forensic-databases.html>
("Forensic Databases: Paint, Shoe Prints, and Beyond," The United States Department of Justice)

Bodziak, W.J. *Footwear Impression Evidence.* CRC Press, 1995.

Identifying Shoe Prints
Skill-Building Activity

Shoe print evidence can be as important as fingerprints in solving a crime. Standard police procedures include taking shoe print samples from the crime scene and suspects. Investigators know the sole or tread pattern of a shoe can reveal many clues about the perpetrator of a crime. Forensic scientists can determine the approximate shoe size, walking style, weight, and height of a person by analyzing his or her shoe prints. The print can be examined to identify the type (running shoe, sandals, sports shoe, or dress shoe), style name, and manufacturer of the shoe. Forensic scientists look for accidental characteristics (scuffs, cuts, scratches, and nicks) that form a unique pattern in the shoe tread. The indentifiable characteristics of a suspect's shoe print and the crime scene evidence can be compared to prove a suspect's innocence or guilt.

Forensic scientists have identified three types of shoe prints: patent, plastic, and latent.

- patent print: a visible print left on a surface from tracking through a material such as mud, blood, or paint
- plastic print: a print left in something soft enough to create a three dimensional impression
- latent print: a print invisible to the naked eye, left on a surface from tracking through a layer of oil and grime

The officers arriving first at the crime scene secure the area. They make a list of people who had access to the scene. This will help to eliminate legitimate shoe prints found at the crime scene: victims, witnesses, police officers, and others with a reason to be at the site. After shoe print evidence has been discovered, it is the job of the investigator to recover and preserve the evidence for analysis. Each type of print is collected using a different method. Investigators photograph patent prints. A cast is made of plastic prints. Latent prints are dusted with powder and lifted with a special adhesive paper.

At the forensic lab, the prints collected by investigators are compared to the suspect's prints. The shoe print is entered into a computer using a scanner or a digital camera. The computer program searches through a shoe print database to determine the manufacturer, make, and model of the shoe. The accidental characteristics are identified. Scientists are able to measure, analyze, and compare the crime scene print to the suspect's print. Using this information, the forensic scientist is able to draw a conclusion about the suspect's shoe and the crime scene evidence.

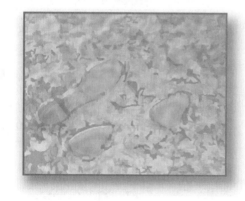

Name: _____   Date: _____

Patent Print Lab
Skill-Building Activity

Purpose: create and compare patent prints

Materials Needed:
- four different types and sizes of old shoes
- paint brush
- ruler
- white paper
- black tempera paint

Procedure:

Step 1: Paint the bottom of a shoe with the black tempera paint.

Step 2: Press the shoe onto the white paper.

Step 3: Lift the shoe off the paper.

Step 4: Let the shoe print dry.

Step 5: Examine the shoe print. Record your observations by completing the data table below.

Step 6: Repeat with the other three shoes.

Patent Print Data Table

Identifiable Characteristics	Shoe #1	Shoe #2	Shoe #3	Shoe #4
Type: sport, dress, sandal				
Brand				
Length (cm)				
Accidental Characteristics: scuffs, nicks, scratches				
Sketch of Shoe Print				

Vandalism
Student Investigation

Crime Scene

Fairfield Police Department officers were called to the Hoover Middle School shortly after 6 A.M. on Tuesday. Someone had vandalized the school's fleet of buses. Officers found that 27 buses had been spray-painted, and windows had been broken in some of them. Officials said the perpetrator didn't sign his or her name, but had left behind the next best thing: partial shoe prints. Police found shoe prints in the sand and a glove on the ground nearby.

Although no other damage was done to the buses, the police said some ignition keys may be missing. The offenders focused primarily on property destruction. Officials reported a preliminary estimate of the damages to be hundreds of dollars. The police believe what may have started as a prank was now a felony offense (a crime which may be punishable by imprisonment). The police are focusing their investigation on Hoover Middle School students because they believe acts of vandalism are most commonly committed by youths between 12 and 14 years old.

School officials told the local newspaper that the act of vandalism was committed sometime before students and staff returned from the Memorial Day weekend. Principal Sands said that vandalism to school property in Fairfield was relatively rare. The vandals had caused enough damage to force Superintendent Dennis Mayberry to cancel school for the day. However, parents were notified that students would need to make up the missed day in the near future. He apologized for the inconvenience and asked anyone with information to call Crime Stoppers or the local police. Who is responsible for the vandalism?

Suspect Information
1. Alex is a seventh-grade student. He won second place at the art show for his spray paint mural.
2. Callie is an eighth-grade student and the student body president. She works at her father's paint store on weekends.
3. Marcus is an eighth-grade student. He is often sent to the principal's office for drawing detailed pen art on his and other student's arms.
4. Sabrina is a sixth-grade student. She was recently suspended from school for drawing on the bathroom walls.

Investigation Directions
Vandalism plagues almost every community in the country. It presents special challenges for law enforcement and takes a variety of forms: broken windows, graffiti, and destruction of property.

Step 1: Read the Investigation Report page.
Step 2: Complete the Shoe Print Analysis Lab page.
Step 3: Use the evidence from your investigation to identify the prime suspect.

Investigation Report

Suspect Statements

People suspected of a crime are asked to give a statement. The statement often reveals the suspect's connection with the crime, where they were at the time of the crime, and a possible motive for committing the crime.

Alex: "I am a spray paint artist. I paint on poster board. My art is different than graffiti. Graffiti is painted on buildings, walls, or trains."

Callie: "I help my dad out on weekends at the paint store. I wasn't able to go on our class field trip because I had to work. I tried to get our sponsor to change the date so I could attend, but she told me it was impossible to make special arrangements for just one student."

Marcus: "I want to be a tattoo artist when I get out of school. I hang out at the Body Art Shop on weekends and pick up pointers on how to improve my designs. Everyone loves my artwork except my teachers."

Sabrina: "My dream is to become a famous artist and paint murals on buildings in New York. No one at this school appreciates my artwork. I was suspended for trying to brighten up those crummy old bathroom walls."

Investigator's Notes

A detective locates and questions witnesses about persons seen or believed to have been in the area at the time of the crime. Observations, descriptions, and identifications made by witnesses can be useful in solving a crime. Investigators evaluate a witness's information and compare it with the related data they have gathered.

Witness #1 Bus Driver: "Alex usually stops by Fridays after school to see if he can help clean the buses for some extra cash. We didn't need any help, so I sent him on his way."

Witness #2 Crime Stopper Volunteer: "Sunday night, I caught Callie in an alley near the school with a plastic grocery bag. I could see she had several cans of spray paint in the bag. I called her parents and waited with her until they arrived."

Witness #3 Store Clerk: "I sold Marcus's older brother several cans of spray paint Saturday night."

Witness #4 Student: "Sabrina was pretty upset about being suspended from school Friday. She told everyone that no one could stop a great artist, and she planned to get even."

Shoe Print Analysis Lab

A shoe print can tell investigators a lot about the person who left it behind. When a criminal tracks through soil, snow, or sand, a shoe impression can be left behind. An impression is a copy made when an object presses into something soft.

An impression can be lifted from the ground by making a cast of it. First, investigators remove lightweight debris which has fallen into the impression using tweezers. Then, hairspray or wax is sprayed on the impression to hold loose soil particles together during the casting process. Next, a cast is made by slowly pouring a casting material into the impression and allowing it to harden. Plaster of Paris and dental stone are two materials often used to make casts. A cast is allowed to dry for 24 to 48 hours before being removed from the ground.

Purpose: compare a plaster cast of the crime scene shoe print to the shoe of each suspect

Materials Needed:
four different types of shoes
    (each labeled with a
    suspect's name)
two shoe boxes with the
    bottom cut out
plaster of Paris
water
spoon
disposable plastic container
hairspray

Procedure:

Step 1: Prepare the plaster of Paris in a disposable plastic container. Follow the directions on the package.

Step 2: Go outdoors and locate the crime scene shoe print.

Step 3: Place the shoe box over the print. Press the box into the mud.

Step 4: Lightly cover the print with hairspray.

Step 5: Slowly pour the plaster mixture into the print until the mixture completely covers the top of the print and meets all four sides of the shoe box.

Step 6: Allow the print to dry.

Step 7: When the print is dry, remove by placing your fingers evenly along the cast's length and inserting them into the soil underneath the cast. Gently lift up. Brush away any dirt and debris.

Step 8: Compare the crime scene print to each suspect's shoe print. Record the information on the Shoe Print Data page.

Name: _____   Date: _____

Shoe Print Data Sheet

Directions: Examine the two casts and the sole of each suspect's shoe. Look for any identifiable features and/or accidental characteristics. Record the information in the data table. Analyze the information to determine which suspect's shoe matches the print found at the crime scene.

Prints	Type (sport, dress, sandal)	Brand	Length (cm)	Accidental Characteristics (scuffs, nicks, scratches)	Sketch of Shoe Print
Crime Scene Print #1					
Crime Scene Print #2					
Suspect #1: Alex					
Suspect #2: Callie					
Suspect #3: Marcus					
Suspect #4: Sabrina					

Whodunit?

Who is the prime suspect in the vandalism case? Use evidence and details from the investigation to support your conclusion.

CASE SOLVED

_____

_____

_____

_____

Case #10
Felony

Science Skills

classify
compare
predict
interpret data
draw inferences

Teacher Information

Crime Location: A girls' restroom at the middle school is the crime scene.

Crime: Someone made a bomb threat.

Investigation: Students compare the similarities and differences in lip prints.

Time Required: The student investigation takes approximately two 50-minute sessions to complete.

Materials Needed

- Skill-Building Activity pages and Student Investigation pages for each student
- See the Lip Print Identification Lab and Lip Print Analysis Lab pages for a list of materials needed for the lab

Teacher Notes

1. <u>Skill-Building Activity</u>: Guide students through the Lip Print Characteristics and Lip Print Identification Lab activity pages.

2. <u>Crime Scenario</u>: Students read and discuss the Crime Scene, Suspect Information, and Investigation Directions found on the Felony: Student Investigation page.

3. <u>Investigation</u>: Divide the class into teams. Instruct each team to read and discuss the information found on the Investigation Report page. Next, students complete the Lip Print Analysis Lab and Lip Print Data Sheet pages. (The lab requires the teacher to provide each team with six lip print cards. Choose four students with different lip print characteristics to help prepare the cards. Instruct each student to apply red lipstick. Then, fold an index card in half, place it in their mouths, and press on it with their lips. Collect the cards, and label each card with a suspect's name. Instruct two of the students to each prepare another lip print card. Label one card Crime Scene Print #1 and the other Crime Scene Print #2).

4. <u>Solve the Crime</u>: Students use the evidence to identify the prime suspect. Teams present their conclusions. There isn't one "correct" answer. The cases are purposely designed to allow students to formulate different plausible solutions based on their interpretations of the evidence.

NSES Science as Inquiry: Content Standard A:
As a result of activities in grades 5–8, all students should develop abilities necessary to do scientific inquiry.

Resources

<http://mac10.umc.pitt.edu/u/FMPro?-db=ustory&-lay=a&-rmat=d.html&storyid=.7933&-Find>
("Dental school researchers study lip prints," University of Pittsburgh)

Harris, Elizabeth Snoke. *Crime Scene: Science Fair Project.* Lark Books, 2006.

Name: _____ Date: _____

Lip Print Characteristics
Skill-Building Activity

One of the first things investigators look for at the scene of a crime is prints: fingerprints, footprints, tire prints, and even lip prints. Lips, like fingers, have special features that are unique to the individual making the print. Like fingerprints, no two lip prints are exactly the same. Therefore, a lip print can be used to identify an individual. Forensic scientists can use lip prints to identify victims or suspects involved in a crime. The study of lip prints is known as cheiloscopy.

An investigator can lift the lip print from a crime scene and take it to the lab for evaluation. When lifting the print, the investigator spreads talcum powder over the print with a soft brush. After the print is photographed, the print is transferred to a piece of clear plastic tape. A piece of tape is placed over the print and then lifted or peeled away. This transfers the lip print to the tape. This print can then be transported to the lab, where it is compared with lip prints from suspects.

Based on the grooves or lines that appear on a person's lips, forensic scientists have identified five basic types of lip prints. Many people's lip grooves or lines are a combination of these patterns.

Short vertical lines or grooves	
Long vertical lines or grooves	
Diamond shaped grooves	
Branching grooves	
Rectangular shaped grooves	

Directions: Using a mirror, examine your lips carefully. Draw your lip identification pattern on the lip print below. Which type of lip pattern do you have?

Name: _____ Date: _____

Lip Print Identification Lab
Skill-Building Activity

Purpose: identify lip types

Materials Needed:

magnifying glasses

10 volunteers

Procedure:

Step 1: Using a magnifying glass, examine the lips of ten students.

Step 2: In the data table, sketch the lip print of each volunteer you examined.

Step 3: Identify the lip type, and record the information in the data table.

Lip Print Identification Data Table

Student	Sketch of Lips	Classification	Student	Sketch of Lips	Classification
#1			#6		
#2			#7		
#3			#8		
#4			#9		
#5			#10		

Felony
Student Investigation

Crime Scene

The Boonville Police Department received a call from Superintendent Nancy Kelly's office at 10:30 A.M. reporting a bomb threat at the Winston Middle School. Students were evacuated and school was dismissed. Police investigating the call found a bomb threat scrawled on a wall in the girl's restroom. Two sets of red lip prints were also found. Someone had kissed the wall near the scrawled threat and the bathroom mirror.

Principal Mills reported to investigators that a student found the threatening message and brought it to the attention of a seventh-grade social studies teacher at 10:15 A.M. This prompted the superintendent to notify local law enforcement and instruct the staff to evacuate the school's 549 students.

Police and firefighters searched the building and found no sign of a bomb. The police chief made the decision to bring in a specially-trained unit of the state police to sweep through the school with a bomb-sniffing dog. No explosive materials were found, and the search ended about 3 P.M.

The next day, school administrators checked the bags and backpacks of incoming students. The detectives questioned Winston Middle School's staff and students. At the end of the day, an assembly was held. Principal Mills reported to the gathering that investigators believed the bomb threat may have been a prank to get out of school. Even so, it is a felony offense to make a false bomb threat. The police made it clear that the student responsible for the incident could face criminal charges and possible jail time. As everyone left the assembly, they were surprised to see four students being detained by the Boonville police. Who is responsible for the false bomb threat?

Suspect Information

1. Caleb is an eighth-grade student and editor of the school newspaper.
2. Jori is a seventh-grade student who loves to play pranks on her friends.
3. Ryan is an eighth-grade student who excels in art class.
4. Lauren is a sixth-grade honor-roll student.

Investigation Directions

Most bomb threats made to schools are pranks, but making a written or verbal threat is considered a serious criminal action. It is a felony offense that could result in imprisonment.

Step 1: Read the Investigation Report page.
Step 2: Complete the Lip Print Analysis Lab page and the Lip Print Data Sheet pages.
Step 3: Use the evidence from your investigation to identify the prime suspect.

Investigation Report

Suspect Statements

People suspected of a crime are asked to give a statement. The statement often reveals the suspect's connection with the crime, where they were at the time of the crime, and a possible motive for committing the crime.

Caleb: "I won the Winston Middle School Journalism Award for my coverage of the Tri-State School Crisis Management Seminar. Afterwards, I tried to point out to our principal that Winston Middle School's crisis plan needed to be updated. Guess I was right."

Jori: "I love to make people laugh. I want to be a comedian some day. Everyone thinks my pranks are funny. Although, my parents didn't think my last prank was so funny and grounded me for a week."

Ryan: "To be a great artist, you have to think outside the box. I entered my Lip Impressions Collage in the Art Fair. It was the talk of the art show even though it didn't win an award."

Lauren: "Being a member of the Winston Middle School Honor Society is a privilege, an honor, and a responsibility. I have to keep a B+ average. I wasn't prepared for the algebra test, so when we were sent home because of the bomb threat, I was relieved."

Investigator's Notes

A detective locates and questions witnesses about persons seen or believed to have been in the area at the time of the crime. Observations, descriptions, and identifications made by witnesses can be useful in solving a crime. Investigators evaluate a witness's information and compare it with the related data they have gathered.

Witness #1 Journalism Student: "At 10:00 A.M., the newspaper staff had a brief meeting. Caleb told us he had proof the school's crisis plan needed to be revised, and he was planning to break the news in the next edition of the school newspaper."

Witness #2 Social Studies Teacher: "At 10:15 A.M., Jori reported the bomb threat message to me. At first I thought it was just another one of her pranks. I went to the restroom and checked for myself. Once I saw the message, I realized I needed to report the incident to the principal."

Witness #3 Art Teacher: "At 10:05 A.M., I gave Ryan a hall pass to use the restroom. He was working on another one of his crazy lipstick projects just before he left the room."

Witness #4 Science Teacher: "Lauren's hair, clothes, and makeup are always perfect. At 10:10 A.M., I saw Lauren leave the girls' restroom. She was carrying her binder and a purse."

Lip Print Analysis Lab

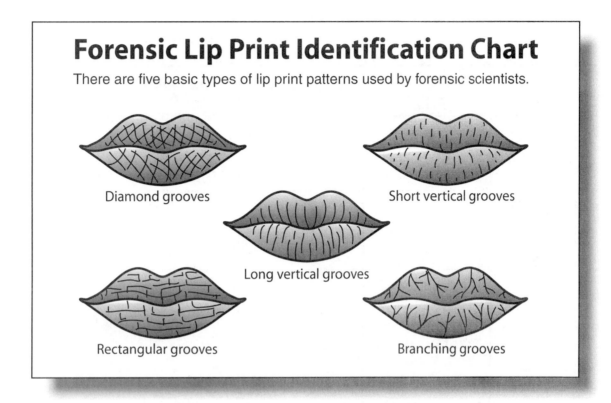

Forensic Lip Print Identification Chart

There are five basic types of lip print patterns used by forensic scientists.

Diamond grooves

Short vertical grooves

Long vertical grooves

Rectangular grooves

Branching grooves

Purpose: compare the similarities and differences in lip prints

Materials Needed:
lipstick print card for each suspect (prepared by the teacher)
crime scene lipstick print cards (prepared by the teacher)
magnifying glass
ruler

Procedure:

Step 1: Use a magnifying glass to examine the lip prints.

Step 2: In the data table on the Lip Print Analysis Data Sheet page, draw each lip pattern.

Step 3: Measure the length and width of each lip print to the nearest millimeter (mm) and record the information on the data table.

Step 4: Classify each lip pattern and record the information in the data table.

Name: _____ Date: _____

Lip Print Data Sheet

Directions: Complete the data table below. Analyze the lip print data to determine which suspect's lip print pattern matches the prints from the crime scene.

Lip Print Data Table

Lip Prints	Sketch of Lip Print	Length in mm	Width in mm	Lip Print Classification
Crime Scene Print #1				
Crime Scene Print #1				
Suspect #1: Caleb				
Suspect #2: Jori				
Suspect #3: Ryan				
Suspect #4: Lauren				

Whodunit?

Who is the prime suspect in the felony bomb threat case? Use evidence and details from the investigation to support your conclusion.

_____

_____

_____

_____

Answer Keys

CSI Crossword Puzzle (page 5)

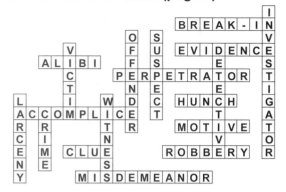

Science Word Search (page 7)

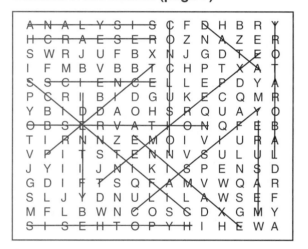

Case #1: Forgery
Handwriting Lab (page 10)
Conclusion: Every person has a unique style of handwriting. Traits will vary.

Handwriting Analysis Lab (page 13)
Whodunit? Four of the suspects' handwriting samples contain similar features found in the permission note: Kathy, Jordan, Amber, and Reilly. Amber and Reilly have the strongest motives for forging the notes.

Case #2: Deception
Truth or Deception Data Sheet (page 17)
Knowing how to interpret body language can help a detective determine if a suspect is being truthful.

Body Language Analysis Lab (page 20)
Whodunit? Jessica and Mrs. Evans both displayed signs of deception when questioned. Their statements revealed they both had a motive.

Case #3: Theft
Fingerprint Analysis Lab (page 27)
Whodunit? Both Mrs. Miller and Kaylee's fingerprints were found at the crime scene. Their statements revealed they both had a motive.

Case #4: Criminal Mischief
Mammal Track Analysis Lab (page 34)
Whodunit? Skunk, squirrel, opossum, and dog prints were found at the crime scene. Madison, Jordan, and Mrs. Martin own dogs. Mr. Scott also has access to dogs and wild animals. All four suspects gave statements that reveal they had a motive.

Case #5: Break-In
pH Analysis Lab (page 41)
Whodunit? Gage and Mikalya both had soil from the crime scene on their shoes. Each gave statements that reveal they had a motive. Each of their alibis placed them near the school during the time the break-in occurred.

Case #6: Burglary
DNA Analysis Lab (page 47)
Whodunit? Breanne and Brittany are twins and have the same DNA. Their DNA matches the crime scene DNA. Each gave statements that reveal they had a motive. Each of their alibis placed them near the school during the time the burglary occurred.

Case #7: Petty Larceny
Chromatography Data Sheet (page 50)
Forensic scientists can use one of the many types of chromatography to identify substances left behind at a crime.

Lipstick Chromatography Data Sheet (page 54)
Whodunit? Answers will depend on how the teacher sets up the lab.

Case #8: Arson
Bite Mark Analysis Lab (page 62)
Whodunit? Matthew's teeth marks most closely match the evidence.

Answer Keys

Case #9: Vandalism
Shoe Print Data Sheet (page 69)
Whodunit? Both Alex and Sabrina's shoe prints were found at the crime scene. Their statements revealed they both had a motive and an opportunity to commit the crime.

Case #10: Felony
Lip Print Analysis Data Sheet (page 76)
Whodunit? Answers will depend on how the teacher sets up the lab.

Bibliography

Bodziak, W.J. *Footwear Impression Evidence.* CRC Press, 1995.

Campbell, Andrea. *Detective Notebook: Crime Scene Science.* Sterling Publishing, 2004.

Levine, Lynn. *Mammal Tracks and Scat.* Heartwood Press, 2007.

Levitt, Irene B. *Brain Writing: See Inside Your Own Mind and Others' with Handwriting Analysis.* The Oaklea Press, 2004.

James, Stuart H. *Forensic Science: An Introduction to Scientific and Investigative Techniques.* CRC Press, 2005.

Reiman, Tonya. *The Power of Body Language.* Simon & Schuster, 2007.

Routh, Debbie. *Learning About DNA.* Quincy, IL.: Mark Twain Media, Inc., 2005.

Saferstein, Richard. *Criminalistics: An Introduction to Forensic Science.* New Jersey: Prentice Hall, 2000.

"Crime and Forensics." 2008. Discovery Communications. 24 Feb. 2008
<http://www.discoverychannel.co.uk/crime/_home/index.shtml>.

"Crime Scene Investigation: A Guide for Law Enforcement January 2000." U.S. Department of Justice. 3 Jan. 2008
<http://www.ojp.usdoj.gov/nij/pubs-sum/178280.htm>.

"Dental school researchers study lip prints." Feb. 7, 2008. University of Pittsburgh. 24 Mar. 2008
<http://mac10.umc.pitt.edu/u/FMPro?-db=ustory&-lay=a&-format=d.html&storyid= 7933& -Find>.

"DNA Forensics." Feb. 21, 2008. U.S. Department of Energy Office of Science. 7 Mar. 2008
<http://www.ornl.gov/sci/techresources/Human _Genome /elsi/ forensics.shtml#1>.

"Forensics In Dentistry." Mar. 14, 2008. American Dental Association. 21 Mar. 2008
<http://www.ada.org/public/topics/forensics_faq.asp>.

"School Vandalism and Break-Ins." Jul. 25, 2005. U.S. Department of Justice. 15 Jan. 2008
<www.cops.usdoj.gov/files/ric/ Publications/School Vandalism BreakIns.pdf>.

"Soil Science Education Home Page." Feb. 12, 2008. NASA. 12 Feb. 2008
<http://soil.gsfc.nasa.gov/>.